The Cheeses

OF VERMONT

The Cheeses

OF VERMONT

A GOURMET GUIDE TO VERMONT'S ARTISANAL CHEESEMAKERS

Henry
Tewksbury

Photographs by Kim Grant

The Countryman Press
Woodstock, Vermont

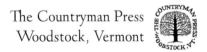

Library of Congress Cataloging-in-Publication Data
Tewksbury, Henry.
The cheeses of Vermont : a gourmet guide to Vermont's artisanal
cheesemakers / Henry Tewksbury. — 1st ed.
p. cm.
Includes index.
ISBN 0-88150-513-7
1. Cheese—Vermont. 2. Cheesemakers—Vermont. I. Title.
SF274.U6 T48 2002
641.3'73'09743—dc21
2001054822

Cover photograph by Laurie Landau, courtesy of the Vermont Cheese Council, www.vtcheese.com
Interior photographs by Kim Grant
Cheese boards courtesy of Snow River Wood Products, Brattleboro, Vermont
Cover and interior design by Dede Cummings Designs
Map on page 204 by Jacques Chazaud, copyright © 2002 The Countryman Press

Published by The Countryman Press, P.O. Box 748, Woodstock, Vermont 05091

Distributed by W.W. Norton & Company, Inc., 500 Fifth Avenue, New York, NY 10110

Printed in the United States of America

10 9 8 7 6 5 4 3 2 1

CONTENTS

Appendixes

Acknowledgments

In addition to the patient and meticulous people at The Countryman Press and the many fine and dedicated cheesemakers of Vermont, I would like to thank all the employees of the Brattleboro Food Coop for their unflagging support, as well as the many cheese lovers on the other side of the counter for their steady encouragement. Special thanks to my son Joshua for keeping the computer operating, and to the center of my home and heart, Cielle, for a thousand and one quiet assists.

Henry the Cheeseman

INTRODUCTION

VIRTUALLY WITHOUT FANFARE and almost by accident, Vermont has in the past six or eight years emerged as the nation's number one producer of farmstead cheeses. While California, Wisconsin, New York, Oregon, and Massachusetts all have several excellent farmstead cheesemakers, Vermont has almost as many as all of them combined.

This book has come about because of these excellent cheeses and the people who make them. As part of one of the largest cheese departments in New England, which carries most of the Vermont-made cheeses, it has been my privilege to explore in depth the subtleties of these exquisite products and to deal personally with all the people who make them. I know the cheeses and I know the people. Hence, it was inevitable that I write this book.

Besides, I have a long history with cheese. I well recall my first involvement more than thirty years ago. In an attempt to bring my two children up in a natural setting where they would learn by personal experience where things come from, my wife and I bought a farm in Vermont. We bought a cow, and eventually learned how to hand milk her in less than an hour. But even a little Jersey cow gave much more milk than our small family could drink. So we made butter with a hand churn. Still too much milk.

"How about making cheese?" my wife suggested.

I bought a how-to book on cheesemaking and plunged in. It was a hideously disorganized volume, with page after page of contradictory instructions. But I finally figured out enough to make many lumpy little wheels of Cheddar, all waxed and aging in my basement. When we finally decided that they had aged long enough to eat, we all assembled to stage a triumphant opening ceremony. The first cheese was terrible: It was moldy under the wax, sour, and quite inedible. So was the second, and the third, and the fifty-third. That ended my career as a cheesemaker. But it began a lifelong fascination with cheese and cheesemaking.

While writing this book has been mainly a labor of love, it has not been without its costs. For example, I will never forget my first meeting with Dan Hewitt. I heard about him from Larry Faillace, whose family makes cheese in Warren, Vermont. He suggested I call "Dr. Dan," as he is known in the tiny town of Granville where he lives, "because he has some sheep and is planning to make cheese."

I called Dan and arranged to pay him a visit to talk about his plans and to meet his animals. I borrowed my ancient mother-in-law's Ford Taurus, which she was no longer able to drive, and headed up Route 100 into the Mad River Valley on a bright crisp morning in late October. Dan was not at his farm in Granville, so I called him at his home a few miles away.

"Come on up," he said in his cheerful English accent and gave me careful directions to his house.

After a couple of false starts I found his road. It was a typical narrow country lane running up a fairly steep hill. Its dirt surface was obscured by the light snow that had fallen the night before. Since it was the first snow of the year, it had not been plowed. I stared thoughtfully at it for some time but finally decided that nothing ventured, nothing gained, and gunned the heavy Taurus up the hill. After about 100 yards, I rounded a blind corner, skidding a little in the 2 or 3 inches of snow, to find myself staring at an old pickup truck heading downhill. Both of us slammed on our brakes and turned our wheels, which had no effect on the two vehicles whatsoever. With a sickening crunch they slid inexorably into each other. I had met "Dr. Dan" all right, head-on.

When I didn't show up at his house, he had come looking for me. Fortunately neither I nor his rugged old truck was hurt, so he kindly took me up to his house while the local tow truck towed my mother-in-law's totaled Taurus to his garage a few miles away. The good thing was that I got my interview with him in the front seat of his pickup while he retrieved his son from day care and drove his daughter to her dance lesson in Montpelier, dropping me at the bus station on the way. The best things in life are definitely not free.

It is a given that all good cheesemakers are obsessed. They are obsessed with time. They are obsessed with temperature. They are obsessed with moisture and texture and appearance. "What are those little brown spots?" they will exclaim in alarm at the appearance of the slightest discoloration. "Do you think they are mites? Should I wipe all the wheels with vinegar? Or wine? Maybe some wine would help."

What's more, they go on being obsessed. As the months and years go by, the more obsessed they become. That's one reason so many cheesemakers work with their partners. They would have a hard time staying together if they didn't. Most of all, they are obsessed by taste.

"What d'ya think?" they will ask after giving you a sample of their latest creation. "Is it too salty? Not salty enough? What about the back of the mouth? Maybe it's too obvious a cheese—too crumbly—too sour . . ." and on and on.

While there are long stretches of Zen-like tranquility during the process of making the cheese, these are often canceled out by the anxiety that attends the aging and marketing part of the profession. All of us cheese freaks should be eternally grateful for their sleepless nights. If they were ever to become complacent about their work, I'm sure the quality of their products would suffer.

There are several fine farmstead cheesemakers here in the Northeast that I have not included in this book simply because they are not located in Vermont. Hillman Farm, where Carolyn Ayotte makes several stunning goat cheeses that are different from but every bit as fine as the best in Vermont, is situated in Colrain, Massachusetts, just over the Vermont state line. Jane North has been making first-class sheep cheese for many years at Northland Dairy in northern New York State, while Old Chatham Sheepherding Company makes the finest Camembert in the country at the nation's largest sheep dairy, also in New York State. In Warwick, Massachusetts, Chase Hill Farm put out its first wheels of Colby in September 2001, and Boggy Meadows Farm, just across the river from Vermont's southeastern border, makes a successful Baby Swiss called Fanny Mason.

While this book is meant to be informative and entertaining, I have written it mainly to honor the dedicated, often inspired, always creative farmstead cheesemakers who have raised an ancient and revered profession far beyond the levels achieved in the centuries past. They lead rich lives and add richness to the lives of others.

The barn at Cobb Hill Farm in Hartland Four Corners

CHAPTER 1

How Vermont Has Become the Leader of the Specialty Cheese Market

NOT LONG AGO THE STATE OF VERMONT WAS synonymous with maple syrup. In less than a decade, however, the state has catapulted to the top of the specialty cheese business in this country. When cheese and maple syrup are mentioned to strangers, 9 times out of 10 their responses are the same: Vermont. Of the 40 cheesemakers in this state, 28 of them make more than 100 cheeses on their own farms from the milk of their own animals. These cheeses that are made from start to finish on the same farm are called farmstead cheeses.

Why Vermont? How did this happen so quickly? Start with its long history as a dairy state. Only half a century ago, most of

Vermont's medium-sized towns were each surrounded by 40 or 50 working farms. At that time, using only hand milking, the state produced 1.3 billion pounds of milk each year from 11,019 farms. Only Wisconsin matched those figures. Today, with sophisticated milking equipment and improved feed, the state is putting out more than 2.6 billion pounds a year from fewer than 1,540 farms.

These days no average town has more than two or three resident dairy farms nearby, and most of them are feeling the pinch of steadily rising costs. Property taxes run between $4,000 and $6,000 a year, steep even with special agricultural allowances. Feed costs have more than quadrupled, and when a tractor can cost nearly $35,000, new equipment is out of the question for the average family farm. The cost of fuel has more than doubled in the past two decades, and labor has virtually priced itself out of existence.

Searching for strength in numbers, most dairy farmers today belong to coops. In New England the well-known Dairy Compact attempts to guarantee farmers that they won't go broke, no matter how low the price of milk goes. It works like this: The price of milk is set by a federal administrator in the U.S. Department of Agriculture. Under normal conditions the farmer will receive plus or minus 28¢ per quart for his milk. By skimming a few pennies off the top of all income, the Dairy Compact sets up a reserve fund. When the price dips below $14 per 100 pounds, it uses the fund to make up at least some of the difference.

Even with this safety net, however, most dairy farm families are living well below the poverty line. Many are investigating ways to raise their income by adding value to their milk. A few have returned to the practice of selling their product in glass bottles in order to tap in to the current mass nostalgia for the good old days when the milkman delivered milk to your house, his bottles clinking reassuringly in the early dawn.

The work of Vermont's 28 farmstead cheesemakers has attracted international attention. Many of their products have found their way on to the gourmet cheese boards of New York City, London, and Paris. In the meantime two of Vermont's oldest nonfarmstead producers have closed up shop in the past year. Butch Seward locked the doors on his sprawling old Seward Family Cheese Facility, and the last piece of Plymouth Cheese was sold a year ago (see chapter 4). The old-style cheesemaker may be giving way to the new breed of farmer/cheesemaker.

Most of these newcomers have been making cheese for only the past five or six years. They don't fit the image that the word *farmer* brings to mind. Ranging in age from 14 to 58, many of them hold graduate degrees from prestigious universities. One is principal of an elementary school. They're sharp businesspeople, expert problem solvers, protective of the environment, and without exception they love their animals. These are hardworking, literate people who are doing what they want to do and doing it well.

Their success is due not only to this commitment but also to the nearly miraculous coincidence of several strongly motivated individuals located in unlikely places. Paul Kinstedt, for example, a professor of dairy science at the

University of Vermont, used to teach large-scale scientific cheese-making. There are four large-scale cheesemakers in Vermont, each making from 30 to 40 million pounds of cheese every year. All of them are fully automated and operate around the clock nearly every day of the year. They are run by engineers and technicians, many of whom are graduates of Professor Kinstedt's classes. During the past six or seven years, however, the professor has developed a personal passion for small-batch farmstead cheesemaking. Since then he has dedicated much of his time to helping Vermont's farmstead cheesemakers create suitable products and apply appropriate scientific knowledge to their production. No one has devoted more time and energy toward building Vermont's reputation for high-quality artisanal cheeses than Paul Kinstedt.

Peter Dixon (see chapter 3) owns no animals and does not live on a farm but has had a strong positive influence on many of Vermont's farmstead cheeses. Now a full-time cheesemaker at Westminster Dairy in Putney, Vermont, Peter grew up on a farm in Guilford. He got his hands into curds and whey as a young boy at the Guilford Cheese Company, his family's business. He now makes distinguished cheeses of his own at Westminster Dairy while organizing and directing quarterly workshops on making various cheeses.

At these workshops, he leads aspiring cheesemakers through the entire process of making cheese. He will often spend several days with interested neophytes in their own kitchens. Using only ordinary household cooking equipment, he shows people how to make many varieties of cheese right on their own kitchen stoves. In this way they can experiment with different recipes until they find one they like before having to invest in the expensive equipment needed to make a salable product. This is 100 percent hands-on learning. Just as there are few, if any, books that can teach you how to write brilliant poetry, paint stunning pictures, or carve memorable sculptures, there is no textbook that can teach you to be a successful cheesemaker. You learn by doing, not by reading.

While these two knowledgeable and dedicated turophiles have been indispensable to the remarkable growth of high-quality cheese in Vermont, the ongoing success story could not have happened without the presence of the right bureaucrat in the right office. Roger Clapp, former Vermont deputy commissioner of agricultural development, used to lean back in his creaking swivel chair, put his hands behind his head, and express a distinctly unbureaucratic opinion: "I see farmstead cheesemaking as a future that is becoming a reality. The future in it is not limitless but it is very encouraging. The number of people going into it is amazing."

Although Roger has moved on to the private sector, he was there at exactly the right time: when Cindy and David Major showed up seeking assistance in realizing their dream of making Vermont's small, stony farms self-supporting. Just before Christmas in 1994, Clapp phoned the Majors on their farm in Putney. A lot of grant money was coming available soon, he said, and he wanted to see a proposal from them on just exactly how they would turn their dream into a reality if given the chance. He wanted it on his desk when he returned from his two-week vacation.

That took care of Christmas at the Major Farm that year.

When Clapp got back from his vacation, on his desk was a proposal from the Majors outlining the Sheep Dairy Center, a small farm on which people interested in becoming cheesemakers could live for six or eight weeks. There they would learn to take care of sheep while they also learned to make the prizewinning Vermont Shepherd cheese that the Majors had created the previous summer (for more on the Vermont Shepherd story, see chapter 3).

Enter Beth Carlson, a young woman from Michigan who joined the Vermont Shepherd family to become this country's first and only *affineuse*. She defines this French word as a woman who takes "a newborn cheese all the way through until it is fully matured." Beth was put in charge of the Major Farm's cheese cave, a large underground room whose temperature and humidity are carefully controlled year-round.

In her first year, Beth took more than 2,000 wheels of Vermont Shepherd cheese through the cave: "By the time it is a month old, I have a pretty good idea what a cheese is going to do." By touching it, lifting it, smelling it, and examining it minutely, she can make a reliable estimate of what is happening inside the wheel, what the moisture content is likely to be, how much longer it will need to stay in the cave before it is mature enough to sell, and even what the quality of the flavor is likely to be.

Beth's experience working at the world-famous Neal's Yard Dairy in London, England, prepared her for the job at Vermont Shepherd's cheese facility. Neal's Yard Dairy is really not a dairy at all. Located in the center of London, this unique company milks no cows and makes no cheese. Instead, representatives scour the countryside of England, Scotland, Wales, and Ireland searching for farmstead cheeses. When they find one that appeals to them they buy as much as the farmer is willing to sell and take it back to their warehouse in the city, where they care for it until they feel it is ready to sell. Beth was in charge of the aging process there.

When she went to work for the Majors, she quickly became the wise-woman of farmstead cheese aging in Vermont and spent much of her time helping new cheesemakers get started. Though she now lives and works in Chicago, Beth left behind a legacy of cheese caves that she helped design for a number of Vermont's cheesemakers. She is still consulted by telephone on an almost daily basis by many of Vermont's farmstead cheesemakers.

Coincidental with Beth's arrival in Vermont, Allison Hooper (see Vermont

Butter and Cheese Company in chapter 4) spearheaded the creation of the Vermont Cheese Council. Nearly all of the state's cheesemakers belong to the council, which is entirely devoted to solving the problems and marketing the products of its members.

One floor below Roger Clapp's former office, Dairy Marketing Specialist Elisa Clancy, who used to handle the daily business of the Vermont Cheese Council, had her former office. She too has moved on, although she still takes care of the council's business. A firm believer in the absolute necessity of cleanliness in cheesemaking, Elisa credits the *Code of Best Practices* hammered out by the council as the single best contribution to food safety available to any new cheesemaker.

This 82-page booklet lays out in detail just about everything a new cheesemaker needs to know about the process of making cheese. In succinct, abbreviated form, it discusses the importance of acidity, starter cultures, rennet, setting and cutting the curd, scalding (cooking), pitching (the process of letting curds settle to the bottom after separating), stacking (another word for "cheddaring"), and so forth. The bulk of the book deals with methods of recognizing and avoiding any possible contamination that might take place in every facet of farmstead cheesemaking, from the care of the animals and their feed to the plumbing, the tanks, the cooking vats, the storage rooms—in other words, everything up to and including the packaging and shipping of the final product. In the back is a useful appendix of charts and forms that can be used to monitor daily activity and record the exact details of each phase of the process. (For information on how to obtain the *Code of Best Practices* see Resources and Information in the appendixes.)

In some states, the department of agriculture is considered an adversary by farmers and cheese producers. In Vermont, the department is a big brother, a positive resource. Byron Moyer, chief of the Dairy Section, and Greg Lockwood, Doug Marsden, and Steve Nicholson, three of the seven dairy inspectors who have the most contact with the farmstead cheesemakers, are demons about following regulations governing dairy operations and cheese facilities, but they are also human and resourceful. As long as a cheesemaker is willing to work with them, they will bend over backward to find alternative but acceptable methods of accomplishing what is necessary.

Rounding out the cast of supporting players in the ongoing drama of Vermont cheesemaking are the various farmer's markets, food coops, and distributors that have gone out of their way to promote Vermont products and to carry Vermont cheeses. Farmer's markets provide ready access to a loyal and increasingly sophisticated customer pool for more than five months of the year. The Brattleboro Food Coop, the Upper Valley Food Coop in White River Junction, Hunger Mountain Coop in Montpelier, Buffalo Mountain Food Coop in Hardwick, Putney Food Coop, and the Onion River Coop and Cheese Traders in Burlington, all use creative marketing techniques to keep these new Vermont cheeses in the spotlight by drawing on the resources of the local distributors (see Resources and Information in the appendixes). Provisions International of White River Junction puts immense effort into picking up and placing farmstead cheeses in Vermont markets; Northeast Coop, headquartered in Brattleboro, sends the Vermont cheeses throughout the eastern United States; Black River Produce outside Ludlow makes it possible for a number of small producers to reach wider markets; and Hillcrest in the northwestern part of Vermont delivers products throughout the state and beyond.

Without the daily contributions of all these people and places, few of the accomplishments of the Vermont artisanal cheese industry would have been possible. This remarkable convergence of talented and committed cheesemakers with the infrastructure that supports them has achieved international recognition in less than a decade. Today their cheeses can hold their own against the artisanal cheeses of France, England, Switzerland, Spain, and Italy.

If there is a secret ingredient at the heart of this phenomenal success story, it can be expressed in one word: *cooperation*. If Joanne James of Lake's End Cheese has a problem with a batch of her cheese, she calls Peter Dixon or Paul Kinstedt, or Marjorie Susman at Orb Weaver. If she needs a certain size valve or a piece of used equipment, she calls Byron Moyer at the department of agriculture. She'll get answers and free advice wherever she turns. These people are in the business of helping each other to succeed. To an amazing degree, they have accomplished their aim.

Peaked Mountain Farm

Fresh Mozzarella is made by hand at Westminster Dairy

CHAPTER 2

How to Make Cheese

IN ORDER TO MAKE YOUR OWN FARMSTEAD CHEESE from the milk of your own animals, you will need to build a cheese facility. This consists of an arrangement of small rooms usually located as close as possible to the animals you will be milking.

The Dairy Section of the Vermont Department of Agriculture has a long list of requirements for cheese facilities. Novice cheesemakers work hand in glove with the state's dairy inspectors from the first pencil sketches to the finished structure. Your cheesemaking facility need not be large, but it must contain at least the following rooms: The cheese room, where the cheese is actually made. A cooling room, where the milk is kept before it goes into the cheese room. A brining room, where the new cheese is submerged in a salt solution. An aging room, where the temperature and humidity are constant. And a production room, where you package your product for shipping and in which you will probably have your office.

Then there is the equipment that goes into your facility. The state dairy inspectors are equally fussy about that and about the way it is hooked up. Only certain types of pipe and pipe joints are allowable. At the least you will need the following items: A cheese vat in which the milk is heated to the proper temperature and in which your cheese will actually be formed. If you intend to make and sell a "fresh" cheese—that is, one that is not aged at least 60 days—you will need a pasteurizer, which is expensive and hard to find. Then, because cheese vats are usually heated by hot water or steam in a jacket that surrounds the vessel, you will need a ready supply of hot water or steam. If you intend to store your milk for a couple of days before making cheese, as most cheesemakers do, you will need a refrigerated bulk tank whose size depends on the amount of milk you need to store. Goats and sheep, for example, give far less milk than cows, and hence require much smaller storage tanks.

Once these minimum requirements of structure and equipment are under way, you can begin to consider what kind of cheese you want to produce. There are several varieties from which to choose, differentiated mainly by the bacterial culture that is used to start them. For example, Cheddar, Monterey Jack, Stilton, Edam, Gouda, Muenster, blue, and many other hard cheeses are all started with mesophilic. This mixture of selected bacteria can be bought as a powder that can then be frozen for up to two years.

But, you say, how can one mixture of bacteria produce seven well-known and distinctive cheeses? Simple. Add another bunch of bacteria at the right time and temperature. It's all there in the recipe you are following. You want Cheddar? Don't add anything but mesophilic. You want Stilton? Add *Penicillium roqueforti* at the right time, in the right amount. (You can't make Stilton for sale, however, because it is *name controlled* (see Glossary), meaning that it is protected by the British government, which will cheerfully confiscate every little glob of Stilton you have just made if you try to sell any of it.)

Every kind of cheese has a recipe. If you're making Gorgonzola, for example, you start with the mesophilic culture. After the curds have drained and become partly dry in the mold, you inject *Penicillium roqueforti.* If you've chosen the right consistency of the partly dried cheese, if the temperature is just right, and if you have the patience to wait four to six months, you will have the satisfaction of seeing the blue-veined interior when you open the wheel. Sometimes, in fact, the blue waits until the air strikes the inside before exploding in startling rays throughout the wheel. If you're even a little bit late or a little bit early, or too warm or too cold, it won't happen, and your pigs will get a great meal of almost Gorgonzola. The process is simple but ever so delicate.

The names of many types of cheese are purely arbitrary and probably came into being more or less by chance. Perhaps some peasant in the third century, who had a few cows in the high Alps, accidentally happened to make some great cheese out of his milk. Pleased with his results and wanting to share it, maybe he yelled over to his neighbor on the next mountain: "Hey, Hans Peter, you want some cheese?"

"What kind?" his neighbor might have yelled back.

"I don't know," the peasant might have replied. "We could call it Gruyère because that's where we are."

Ever since then, cheese from that region of Switzerland has been called Gruyère. Over the centuries since then, clever and committed cheesemakers have experimented tirelessly until they have put together a neat and reliable recipe that can be used anywhere in the world and called Gruyère, even in Hoboken, New Jersey, or Davenport, Iowa.

Swiss cheese originated in several places throughout Switzerland and because of that still bears the generic name: Swiss. Its flavor varies from country to country, even from town to town, but it starts out with the same two cultures: thermophilic for taste and *Propionibacter shermanii* to produce the gas that in turn causes the familiar holes to form.

All of the general categories of cheese differ from one another in part because of the bacterial culture they start with. (Many other factors, including moisture and acidity, also come into play.) All blue cheese gets a shot of *Penicillium roqueforti*. In the Middle Ages and before, it was thought to be powerfully medicinal and used as a cure for many illnesses. Without knowing what it was, the people of that time had discovered penicillin. The outside surface of Brie and Camembert is dusted with *Penicillium candidum* so that the cheeses cure from the outside toward the center. Cheddar, Monterey Jack, Stilton, Edam, Gouda, and Muenster all start with a mesophilic culture, while Feta and some blue cheeses get jump-started with Flora Danica. Like Swiss, all Parmesans, Mozzarellas, and Provolones use an Italian thermophilic culture to get the process rolling. Only after the curds have been separated from the whey and the liquid mostly drained off do they take separate paths through the cheesemaking process, until they reach the destination the cheesemaker has chosen.

Even today, many cheeses of the world do not belong to any of these categories. The recipe is unique to the maker and is named at the whim of the cheesemaker. Here in Vermont, Middletown Cheese is named after the farm in Londonderry where it is made. Crowley Cheese in Healdville is named for the man who started it, and Orb Weaver takes its name from the farm outside Middlebury where it is made. Indeed, you may have no idea what kind of cheese you are making when you first begin. Keep careful records and try first one culture and then another, or a combination of the two, or perhaps just a helping of pure yogurt or a cup of yesterday's milk that has begun to sour. When you find one you like, try to duplicate it. If you're lucky, it will become your own special cheese, and you can name it anything you want to.

Large factory cheesemakers maintain research and development departments that are constantly seeking to create new and different products. But despite all their fancy equipment and scientific knowledge, it is still possible to come up with cheese they had no intention of producing. The classic case is Parrano. Holland has been famous for Gouda for centuries, but when one of their largest factories decided to develop an Italian cheese, what they ended up with was Parrano, an excellent cheese that tastes like aged Gouda with overtones of smoked Mozzarella, Gruyère, and Parmesan floating through it. Since it really wasn't any of the above, they invented the name Parrano. Perhaps someday other Parranos will appear in other places, and it will carve its own niche in the pantheon of the cheese gods along with Cheddar, Swiss, and Mozzarella.

Now let's presume that the day has finally arrived when your cheesemaking facility is completed and has passed its inspections. You have your equipment installed and ready. You've done enough kitchen stove experiments to decide what kind of cheese you want to produce, and you're ready to make cheese.

Though the steps you need to take seem fairly simple, you will soon discover that there are infinite variations in the process. These variations depend not only on the kind of cheese you have chosen to make, but also on the quality of your milk and the conditions of your local environment. Basically, however, the following is the ritual you have to follow if you wish to make an aged raw milk cheese.

First, you must transfer the milk from the animal to the cheese vat. There are many ways to accomplish this, depending on how close the milking parlor is to the cheese room. Some pour the milk into cans and carry it to the vat. Many

Milking time at Boucher Farm

store a two- or three-day supply of milk in a can cooler before filling the vat, while others have to carry the milk supply in the back of a pickup truck to reach the cheese rooms. One woman hauls her milk from the barn in a child's wagon and, in winter, on a toboggan.

Once the milk is in the vat, you warm it slowly to a temperature of 85 to 92 degrees and stir in your culture. You then do something else for 45 minutes to an hour—shovel snow, feed the baby, make phone calls, lube your car. The time will vary depending on acid production, which varies from day to day and must be closely monitored. When your timer goes off, you add coagulant. A coagulant is a liquid that causes the curds to separate from the whey. You can buy it from the same company that sold you the cultures you are using. (See The Rennet Quandary in the appendixes.) Some cheesemakers stir in the coagulant using large wooden paddles, some do it with a shovel, and many plunge their thoroughly scrubbed-down arms into the warm milk and wave them around madly. Many cheesemakers have CD players in their cheese rooms and wallow around in the

Stirring the curds and whey at Crowley Cheese Factory

Cutting the curd at Shelburne Farms

curds and whey to the strains of everything from Bach to Brubeck. Whatever your method, you keep stirring until you're thoroughly winded and need a break. After a short rest you will discover that the milk has magically transformed into a solid mass the consistency of old-fashioned custard. This is called the curd and, just as in little Miss Muffet's day, you now need to cut it in order to release the whey, a very watery liquid that contains little butterfat. Several ingenious tools are available for cutting the curd. One is a large fan-shaped paddle with thin parallel blades like a bandsaw stretched across the open area about ¾ inch to 1 inch apart. This is passed carefully but relentlessly through the soft curd, first in one direction, and then in another at right angles. Some of the large cheesemakers who need to cut several thousand gallons of curd at one time employ an electrical curd cutter that hangs down from an overhead rail and is propelled slowly from one end of the vat to the other. Many small farmstead cheesemakers simply use a long bread knife with or without a serrated blade.

The cutting transforms the solid curd into approximately 1-inch cubes and releases the whey, which now needs to be drained. You can dip it out with a bucket and pour it onto a whey table, which funnels the liquid into a floor drain, or open a valve in the vat and let it run out the bottom. During this process, you continue to wave your arms around in the curd cubes to keep them from sticking to each other, which they will stubbornly insist on doing if you stop agitating them for even a moment. Of course if you are obsessed enough to make whey butter or whey cheese, such as Ricotta Salata or Myzithra, you save every little drop of the whey for reprocessing at a later time.

Now that you are thoroughly exhausted, you give it up and just let the curds stick together into a warm, irregular solid mass. At this point, if you are making Cheddar, you engage in what is called cheddaring. To accomplish this, you cut the now solid curd into fairly even slabs the size of large pillows. Pile them up two or three deep along the sides of your heated vat, leaving the center open. More whey continues to drain from the slabs as you constantly repile them until you feel that you have slapped as much whey from the slabs as your endurance will allow. The temperature of the curd has been constantly maintained during the above process by adding or cutting off the steam or hot water you have flowing into the jacket surrounding your vat.

After adding whatever amount of salt your recipe calls for, you will now

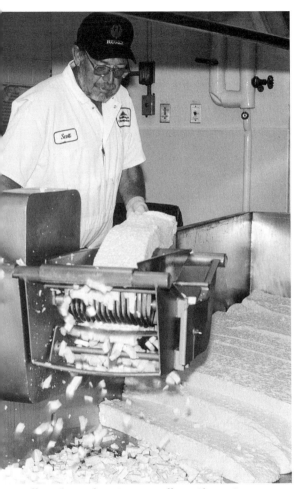

Milling the curd at Grafton Village Cheese Company

mill the curd with an appropriate tool. If you're working in a large vat, you can hang an electric milling machine from the same overhanging track mentioned earlier, and simply load the slabs of curd into the machine as it moves slowly down the length of the vat. You shovel the slabs into a hopper, and a revolving drum covered with knives cuts the curds up into small pieces. You keep them from sticking together by installing moving shafts on the overhead track. These have eccentrically located blades on the bottom and move up and down through the curds, keeping them well separated. Most farmstead cheesemakers mill the curd by hand using a large sharp knife, which is usually the same one they have used to cut the curd in the first place. They then keep the curd agitated by more frantic hand stirring, which of course releases more whey.

If all you want is cheese curd, this is where you stop, because curd is what you

Packing molds at Lakes End

have. You're probably too stubborn to be satisfied with that, however, so you reach for your shovel or your bucket or a large scoop and ladle the curd onto a stainless-steel cheese table that is slanted to let the whey run off. From there you pack it into molds, which come in a large variety of sizes and shapes depending on what you want your cheese to look like at the end. You then press as much whey out as you can. This is usually done by hand with what strength you have left, or in a small-batch endeavor by perforating the bottom of a coffee can that has been fitted with a hand-cut wooden plug or even an appropriate-sized plate. You put a brick or a mason jar of water on the plate and leave it in a cool place overnight.

In the morning your cheese will be dry enough to be removed from the molds, wiped off with a clean cloth, and brined. This consists of plunging the wheels (or blocks or slabs or globs) of cheese into a solution of salt and water, being sure to turn them in the brine at least once. This toughens the rind and makes the invasion of unfriendly fungi and bacteria less likely. Remove them

Brining the cheese at Blythedale Farm

from the brine, dry them again, and place them on clean shelves in whatever area you are using for aging your product.

If you're obsessive enough, you will eventually construct a cave for aging your cheese. You can use your basement, however, as long as it remains moist enough year-round and maintains a constant temperature of about 50 degrees Fahrenheit. Humidity is a critical consideration when curing cheese. Depending on what sort of cheese you are making, the humidity must stay at a constant

level between 85 and 95 percent. For example, soft-ripened cow's milk cheese requires 95 percent humidity to cure properly, while most goat cheese must be kept between 85 and 90 percent for proper ripening.

During this period of aging, you perform the duties of an *affineur* (see the glossary). This requires almost daily turning and constant wiping, or, if you are making a washed-rind cheese, wiping each cheese with a cloth that has been dipped in salt water, vinegar, wine, beer, or whatever you choose. During this phase there is constant examination to forestall the invasion of unfriendly and uninvited bacteria that might

Aging in the cheese cave at Vermont Shepherd

cause pits or small "volcanoes" on the slowly drying rinds. It is an irony of cheesemaking that bacteria are both your best friends and your worst enemies.

These are what are called natural-rind cheeses. You may prefer to dip your cheese in melted wax after you have pressed it, using several coats to prevent mold. It will age slowly in the wax and will not require as much turning or as cool a storage room. You will need to continue playing *affineur/affineuse* for at least 60 days because the law of the land currently stipulates that you may not sell a cheese made from raw milk unless it has been aged for 60 days, which reduces the risk of pathogenic bacteria. Anything aged less than that is considered a fresh cheese and must be pasteurized.

In conducting this process, the cheesemaker consults a parade of temperature readings and pH values in order to know the optimal moment to take each step. It is significant, however, that when asked the question, "Is cheesemaking an art or a science?" all the cheesemakers in this book felt that it was both. Science told them what was probably happening at any given moment, but it took art to know when it was time for the next step.

Ripening cheese is brushed daily in the cave at Vermont Shepherd

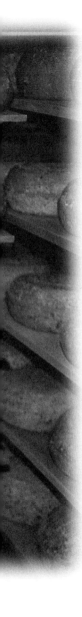

THE
CHEESEMAKERS

Vermont Shepherd cheese is made at Major Farm in Putney.

CHAPTER 3

The Cheesemakers of Southern Vermont

WESTMINSTER DAIRY
Fresh Mozzarella; Traditional Aged Provolone;
Smoked Provolone; Asiago Fresco

If you shopped around for the ideal ingredients for a new cheese facility here in Vermont, you could hardly do better than combine Harlowe's Organic Vegetable Farm in Bellows Falls with Livewater Organic Dairy Farm in Westminster West. That is, until you persuaded Peter Dixon to be your cheesemaker. Hence it is no surprise to find John Slason, Paul Harlowe, and Bill Aquaviva of Harlowe Farm teamed up with Peter Dixon at Livewater Farm outside Putney in a cheesemaking operation they call Westminster Dairy. They started in the summer of 2000 with an organic fresh Mozzarella and an organic Provolone, two cheeses not made in

Vermont at the time. Peter now makes cheese there three times a week.

In a state full of fine cheesemakers, Peter Dixon stands tall. He grew up on a small dairy farm in Guilford. In the early 1980s, his father and stepmother decided to make cheese, so Peter enrolled in a cheesemaking course in Guelph, Ontario. In 1983 they founded the Guilford Cheese Company, one of the first farmstead cheesemakers in the state. They made a simple, mild, farm-style cheese that was quite popular.

In order to expand their operation they went into partnership with Renard Giard, a fourth-generation maker of Brie in France. Giard sent a young French cheesemaker to work for a year with Peter. They built a quarter-million-dollar factory across the road from the farm and began making a Brie and a Camembert that enjoyed a fine reputation in southern Vermont and Massachusetts. Unfortunately, the partnership didn't last. Most merchants of that period were unfamiliar with handling the naturally ripened cheeses that Guilford was making. Eventually it became difficult to market enough cheese to sustain the company's growth.

Peter, who by then had married Hilary, moved to Burlington in order to complete his education. While studying for his master's degree in dairy science, he took both of Paul Kindstedt's cheesemaking courses and spent his summers working with Mariano Gonzales, who was then the cheesemaker at Shelburne Farms. Fresh from college, Peter went to work for Allison Hooper and Bob Reese at Vermont Butter and Cheese Company in Barre (see chapter 4). During

Livewater Farm's Jersey cows provide milk for fresh Mozzarella.

the four years he spent there, he learned all about goat cheese and worked with Allison to develop a quality control program that directly involved all the goat's milk suppliers.

Following that success, Cindy and Dave Major offered Peter an opportunity to develop two new cow's milk cheeses for their company, Vermont Shepherd (see page 35). No deadlines, no strings—he would be on his own as long as his results were compatible with Vermont Shepherd's products. And Vermont Shepherd would age and market the cheeses. In that way, Putney

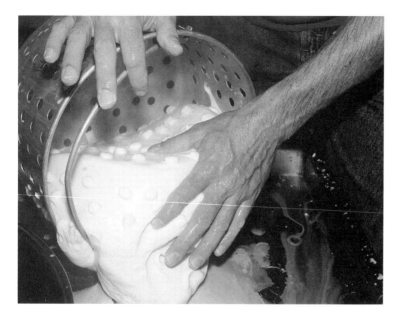

Peter Dixon makes his fresh Mozarrella entirely by hand

Tomme and Timson were born.

Now that Peter has his own facility, he is expermenting in many directions as well as conducting courses in cheese-making several times a year. There is nothing fancy or state-of-the-art about the equipment at Westminster Dairy, but the cheese room is large enough to handle the quantity of milk coming from Livewater's small herd of Jersey cows. The old equipment breaks down from time to time, but it is fully certified and more than adequate to do what it needs to do. The cheese room at Westminster Dairy has a large window through which visitors, who are welcome at the farm, can watch Peter at work. In a basement under the cheese room is a specially designed aging room that combines radiant heating with moisture from above.

Peter makes his own cheese cultures, usually out of yogurt. He feels that he can maintain more personal control of his products that way. Most places that make pulled Mozzarella, as fresh Mozz used to be called, use a machine to form the small pillows of cheese. Peter makes his by hand, squeezing and pulling the curd until it is formed into just the right sizes. After a short period in brine, it is ready for packing into tubs filled with a lower percentage of brine.

The nearly perfect combination of people that have created this facility makes it one of the most exciting farmstead cheesemaking operations in Vermont.

VERMONT SHEPHERD
Vermont Shepherd; Putney Tomme, Timson

The history of Cindy and Dave Major reads like a chapter from Horatio Alger. Pretty, dark-haired Cynthia, the daughter of a New York milk processor who loved to visit dairy farms, went to Marlboro College in Vermont, where at a contradance in her sophomore year she met David, son of a sheep farmer in Westminster West. After surviving a serious bicycle accident, spending 10 days in a coma, undergoing orthopedic surgery, and enduring a two-year recovery, Cindy went to live on David's sheep farm, where they tried to make a living with its lamb and wool operation. Then the babies arrived, and just as she was considering a career in physical therapy, Cynthia's father suggested that they milk the sheep and make cheese. Cynthia picked up a book on sheep dairying at a farm show. David built a one-sheep stanchion. Nearby Putney School had a state license to make cheese. Armed with the necessary equipment, Cynthia and David made cheese at Putney School.

"We kind of made this horrible cheese for a couple of years," she says.

"Put most of it on the manure pile," he adds.

Their first entry to the American Cheese Society's annual judging came in dead last.

To add injury to insult, their first experience with mold nearly put them out of business. Cindy was up at 5 A.M., scrubbing everything down with vinegar: floors, walls, ceilings, equipment. Took her all that day to get rid of it. The next day it all came back.

Faced with a decision either to go somewhere and learn how to do it right or just give it up, Cynthia picked up a copy of *The French Cheese Book* by Patrick Rance, wrote to the author, and asked him where they should go. His answer: "Go to the Pyrenees."

So after writing letters to a number of small sheep farms in southern France, enclosing family and farm photographs, they packed up their small children and went to France. They visited all the people Cindy had written to, people with children like theirs, living on small, hilly farms like theirs. And they learned to make cheese. They learned to put their hands in it. They watched one farmer, whom they nicknamed the Rock 'n' Roll Cheesemaker, milk hundreds of sheep with state-of-the-art equipment and make great cheese, while his father, a more traditional farmer, milked 200 sheep by hand and made his cheese in small gas-fired vats. They discovered that although these farms were using the same cultures in the same area, every one of their cheeses tasted entirely different.

David Major rounds up a flock of errant sheep with the aid of his Border collies.

They figured out that if they were careful with what they produced and didn't try to make large batches quickly, they could turn out cheeses that were consistent in flavor.

As they were leaving, a farmer's wife told them: "You do everything we have told you and you will be great!"

And they were. Their second submission to the American Cheese Society's judging won first prize in the Farmhouse Division and was runner-up for Best of Show. The year after that, they were judged Best of Show for the entire country.

It wasn't roses all the way, however. The first cheeses they made after returning from France were far from prizewinning quality.

"They were all wrinkly," Cindy recalls, "because we didn't know about turning them in the brine, and I just knew they were going to be disasters."

After staring at them for four months with steadily increasing apprehension, she couldn't stand it anymore and snuck down to the cave and cut one of the awful things open.

"It was so good! It was utterly delicious! I just stood there jumping up and down and cut the whole thing up and ran around giving pieces to anyone I could find!"

Vermont Shepherd is the flagship of the rapidly growing Vermont farmstead cheese movement. It operates without a distributor by manipulating scarcity as a marketing device, hand delivering, selling off the farm, and using United Parcel

Service. It has managed to get premium prices for its products in such prestigious outlets as Dean & DeLuca, Zabar's, and Balducci's in New York City, and Formaggio's in Cambridge, Massachusetts. Its cheeses appear on the cheese boards of many fine restaurants as far away as San Francisco and London.

KC's Kritters
Fresh Chèvres; Goat Milk Brie; Goat Feta; Swiss

Kevin Kingsley lives in Guilford on a farm that used to belong to his father-in-law, who now lives across the street. Before he married his wife Kevin used to work for her father, helping him milk his 200 cows. A year after he started work, Kevin married Carolyn, and soon they had three children: Ann, Joshua, and Tristan. After Kevin got kicked in the knee by a heifer and endured four operations, he wasn't much good for milking cows.

In 1989 he bought his first goat. He's still milking her, along with nearly 35 others, a mixed herd of La Mancha, Nubian, and French Alpines. "Got my whole herd in 56 feet square," Kevin boasts. "Couldn't come near that with cows." He found that he could make goat Brie quite easily because his farm happened to be located in an area whose atmosphere is saturated with white mold. "I'd been spraying it on the cheese," he said, "But then I missed some and the mold was on them too."

He uses the same freeze-dried culture from France in all his cheeses. With the Brie, he then sprays a water-based, mold-saturated solution on both sides of the wheel. The mold has no effect until he adds salt. The salt forms a thin skin and warms up the mold, which then grows through the skin and coats the cheese with that familiar soft, fuzzy, white rind. Kevin ripens his Brie in a walk-in cooler built in the corner of the huge, free-stall cow barn. Curd left over from the Brie goes to make Feta, and the whey from all the cheeses is a treat for their pigs.

The Kingsleys got into the cheese business more or less by accident. After Kevin was kicked, they bought a goat in order to have fresh milk. That started him thinking about acquiring a herd and selling the milk to the Vermont Butter and Cheese Company, which was always looking for high-quality goat's milk. He rejected the idea because Barre is a long drive, and because he would need 200 goats to come out ahead financially. So, he read some books and found some basic cheese recipes.

Byron Moyer, head of the Dairy Section of the Vermont Department of Agriculture, told him what he would need to get started. A grant from Vermont Family Farms bought his pasteurizer, and a Small Business Administration loan enabled him to buy 30 goats and the necessary equipment. He and Carolyn decided to use their first initials to name the new company.

Kevin started remodeling at the end of June 1993 and made his first cheese less than two months later. The milking parlor, milk room, cheese plant, and the regulation bathroom were all plumbed and wired. The entire complex of rooms is crammed into a very small barn along with the goats. Without moving more than a few steps, Kevin can reach everything. He milks into buckets and pours them off into a small bulk tank, which has a short pipeline to his pasteurizer and cheese vat. The place is tiny and spotlessly clean.

Distributors had given him letters of intent so that he could get the loan from the Small Business Administration, but when he actually had cheese to distribute, none of them would carry it. He went into the local farmer's market, which eventually led to a contract with what was then Bread and Circus in Whately, Massachusetts, and through them to other Bread and Circuses in New England.

Now, Kevin and Carolyn do all of their own distribution, hand-delivering orders to regular customers on a weekly basis. The whole family shows up at the Brattleboro Farmer's Market every Saturday morning. Once the word of mouth took over, marketing their product was not difficult.

Adversity does seem to be his middle name, however. A small part buried deep in his old separator broke last year, and for more than six months Kevin was unable to make his line of low-fat chèvres. With a new separator running around $20,000, and used ones at $12,000, when Kevin had originally paid only $100 for the broken one, there was only one solution: Find another separator of the same vintage in which the broken part was intact. He eventually found it at a friend's farm, and KC's Kritters once again sells low-fat chèvres.

Although it cost her a broken ankle, Kevin and Carolyn made their own hay this summer with the help of their strong, grown-up children. Kevin is very proud that there are five generations of Kingsleys still engaged in farming.

GRAFTON VILLAGE CHEESE COMPANY

Classic Cheddar; Gold Label Cheddar; Four-Star; Smoked Cheddar; Sage Cheddar; Garlic Cheddar

For more than 30 years, Scott Fletcher, the grand old man of Vermont cheese-making, has been turning out Cheddar at Grafton Village Cheese Company. In the late 1960s Scott, just out of high school, knocked on its front door at the very moment the company was looking for someone young and eager to work. He has been there ever since making some of the finest Cheddar in this country.

Scott was the seventh baby born at the Grace Cottage Hospital in Townshend. When he first went to work at Grafton, he and a man named Ed McWilliam did everything, with a little advice from a professor at the University of Vermont. Today only 2 of the original 44 local dairy farms supply milk to the company. By special arrangement, Agri-Mark, which picks up all the milk for Grafton, brings only guaranteed rBGH-free Jersey milk (see the glossary). The company now employs more than 20 people, one of whom is his wife, Maureen. She manages the little store in the front of this compact, picturesque building. Within walking distance of Grafton Village in the middle of a sizable hay field, it's not hard to find. There's a covered bridge next to the building that has no purpose except to be admired and photographed.

Scott's 10-hour day starts at 5:45 A.M. when he fills the two cheese vats with 13,000 pounds of raw milk each and starts raising their temperature gradually to

82 degrees. After approximately eight hours, Scott and his production manager will have converted 26,000 pounds of milk into 2,600 pounds of Cheddar all packed into molds and ready for aging. The night shift will make another 2,600 pounds.

Scott's whole operation is low-tech and hands-on. For measuring acidity he uses a measuring cup, an acidity tester, and charts. Since time and temperature are important to the process, he is constantly feeling the curd, touching the sides of the vat, and sampling small pieces. It's almost as if the cheese were an extension of himself.

Peter Mohn, vice-president of the Grafton Cheese Company, is fond of saying that Scott "teaches milk how to be cheese." He handles that cheese seven or eight times a day.

The Grafton Village Cheese Company was originally founded in 1890.

By the time he shovels it into molds, which is what he enjoys the most, he knows just about everything there is to know about that batch.

If you were to drive past Grafton Village Cheese Company in the afternoon of a warm July day, you might see two men sitting on the cement curb leaning against the huge bulk tank. They would be drinking coffee or enjoying a snack. One of them would be Scott.

PEAKED MOUNTAIN FARM
Marinated Sheep Feta; Peaked Mountain Tomme; Peaked Mountain Camembert

On top of a steep hill in Townshend, just above a farm that raises bison, Ann and Bob Works own Peaked Mountain Farm, a storybook 100-acre former Morgan horse farm with a huge, beautifully built post-and-beam barn on one side of the road and, on the other side, a large, rambling, impeccably furnished home complete with a talking bird and a great shaggy dog. They have raised four children, all but one of whom has grown up and gone, and they have no immediate background in farming.

Both are passionate about cooking. Bob, who has just finished a successful real estate career in New York City, is out to raise the threshold of the local citizens' appreciation of fine food, gourmet cheese, and vintage wine by endowing a shelf in the Townshend library with a collection of exotic cookbooks and other literary works concerning fine food. These are the last people in the world you could imagine shoveling sheep manure or assisting a ewe with a difficult lambing. But appearances deceive. Not only have they worked 15 hours a day at Major Farm, but Ann has taken Paul Kindstedt's classes at the University of Vermont, read copiously, and attended seminars on animal care and cheesemaking.

"As much as neither one of us knows what we're doing," confesses Bob, "I know even less."

They both came from Minnesota, and for them to take on this challenging project is rather like turning back the clock. Bob's family currently owns a farm in Wisconsin. Also, for two or three centuries the Workses owned and operated Richwall Farm across the Connecticut River in Westmoreland, New Hampshire, a dazzling estate bordered by the river.

The ghosts of their ancestors are looking over their shoulders as they and their dog gather their flock of East Friesian crosses, bought partly from Cindy and Dave Major and watched over and protected from coyotes by their two miniature guardian donkeys called Dis and Dat. The dog funnels the flock into its brand-new milking parlor on the bottom level of the barn. It sits alongside the shiny new milk room, which opens into the bright, airy cheese room with its long wall of windows. Also newly built above the cheese room are two small bedrooms to house the interns they have helping them.

This sea change in the Works' lives all happened because of their admiration of Vermont Shepherd cheese, which they first tasted at the Brattleboro

Ann and Bob
Works with a few
of their East
Friesian crosses

Food Coop. They subsequently read an article in the local paper about Major Farm and the tours that were being offered. Both Ann and Bob went home from the tour in near silence, each privately convinced that somehow they had to be involved in that project, a feeling that each concealed from the other for several days before it exploded and became rapidly transformed into a reality.

"We just want to get a nice cheese out that people can afford," says Bob.

Toward that end, they are experimenting with a sheep Feta as well as trying some cow cheese made with milk from Jesse Pomeroy's Middletown Farm (see chapter 4). Ann milks 60 sheep twice a day throughout the summer, while Bob tends the fields and helps with the cleanup.

They are like a couple of bright-eyed kids fresh out of school and embarked on an adventure over uncharted waters.

Neighborly Farms in Randolph, Vermont

The Cheesemakers of Central Vermont

THE TAYLOR FARM

Vermont Farmstead Gouda; Maple Smoked Gouda

Katie and Jon Wright, a young couple with three young children, lease the Taylor Farm near Londonderry, Vermont. They have much in common with Dawn and Daniel Boucher (see chapter 5). Both farmers are native Vermonters, both couples met on blind dates, both make cheese once a week, both pump raw milk directly into their cheese vats from the milking cows, and both were convinced by watching Marjorie Susman and Marian Pollack at Orb Weaver (see chapter 5) that it was possible to make cheese on a small scale.

Jon used to work the Taylor Farm when he was a teenager. When he and Katie leased it in 1989 it was rather like coming home. He built up the milking herd from a handful of cows to the present 50 head. Even so, it was difficult to make ends meet, especially with three children. They thought about bottling, but after a trip to Shelburne Farms (see chapter 5) and another to Orb Weaver, they began to consider making cheese. The 260-acre farm on both sides of a hardtop, well-traveled main road is perfectly situated for the tourist trade. In the days they operated a roadside stand, more than 6,000 people a year stopped for home-made baked goods, preserves, and such Vermont cheeses as Grafton, Blythedale, and Vermont Butter and Cheese Company. In winter they also take people on sleigh rides pulled by a magnificent matched pair of Belgian workhorses. These days tourists can not only purchase their new farmstead Goudas but actually see them being made.

One of the residents of Taylor Farm

The Wrights' compact, efficient cheese room was designed with the help of Peter Dixon (see chapter 3). He brought his years of experience into their kitchen before they started and spent three days making cheese with them. He also helped them find appropriate equipment and then worked directly with them on the first four batches until they felt confident of their ability to execute the process.

On an average cheesemaking day, Jon scrubs and sterilizes the cheese room before starting the morning milking. Dick, an older man who used to drive a milk truck, starts the process by letting the milk into the cheese vat and raising its temperature to 92 degrees before adding the culture. By the time it has incubated for 45 minutes, Katie has finished getting the kids fed and off to school and joins Dick in time to add the vegetable enzyme they use for coagulation. The rest of the process is much the same as it is for all the other cheesemakers.

They have plenty of room for expansion, but Jon is only half joking when he says that they'll also have to raise 150 pigs to get rid of the whey. As long as the people who own the farm don't decide to sell, Katie and Jon and their children will be there for the long run.

Woodcock Farm
Peabody Hill; Weston Tomme; Piper Hill; West River Sheep Supreme

Question: What do video production and ceramic tile have to do with making cheese? Answer: Normally nothing, but in the case of Mark Fischer in Weston, those are the steps in his life that eventually led him to Vermont and the Major Farm. He and his wife, Gari, decided that 10 years in Manhattan was long enough. Her brother had a second home in Londonderry, Vermont, which sounded to them like a good place to start looking for an alternative lifestyle.

Having no farming experience, they phoned the Vermont Department of Agriculture, asked what the chances were of earning a living on a farm in Vermont. They were told that it would be very difficult because farm real estate in Vermont has priced itself out of sight of a decent return on investment.

But they liked Vermont and decided to take a chance. Mark gave up his video production business in the city, and with his wife and young daughter, Samantha, age three, found a place to rent in the Londonderry area, where he got into selling ceramic tile. A year later their second child, Oliver, was born in Rutland. Three or four years ago, looking for some other activity, Mark happened to run into David Major's brother on a competitive trail ride they were both involved in. They got to talking, the way people on competitive trail rides do, and the subject of cheese came up. Specifically, Vermont Shepherd cheese.

Almost before they knew it Mark and Gari had signed up to apprentice at the Sheep Dairy Center. They fell in love with the whole cheesemaking process, bought 30 acres of empty land in Weston in what used to be a gravel pit, built a bright airy cheese house with lots of room, put up a Quonset-style barn made of metal poles with heavy-duty plastic pulled over them, installed a milking parlor similar to what they had used at the Majors', and, with the help of Peter Dixon, found some good used equipment. So all of a sudden city boy Mark Fischer found himself with 44 East Friesian crossbred sheep, none of which had ever been milked before. He would push the ewes one by reluctant one up the ramp to the stanchions he had installed on the milking platform, cramming each one into the stanchion where she would get her grain, and hand milking each from below while ducking the shower of manure pellets that the nervous ewes produced.

"I kept thinking," says Mark ruefully, "what have I done to myself?"

Somehow, the sheep finally calmed down and learned to make their way peacefully in and out of the milking parlor. A few steps away is the cheese room where the Fischers have made many wheels of excellent Vermont Shepherd cheese.

"The only way to make this really pay," he says, "is to make your own product and age it and wrap it and distribute it yourself, perhaps through a catalog."

While continuing to supply cheese to Vermont Shepherd, the search for a "good product" goes on. With Peter Dixon's help, they have produced an excellent sharp, creamy, Bulgarian-style Feta and a rich, pure white, absolutely delicious cheese they call Peabody Hill. Gari makes this by ladling it into the molds without cutting the curd.

With the nervous humility of people who have deliberately changed their whole existence, the Fischers are now milking between 60 and 70 ewes and trying to find that elusive entity "the perfect farmstead cheese" that everyone will love and no one has yet thought of.

Pomeroy Farm
Jesse's Middletown Cheese

Not far from Woodcock Hill and the Taylor Farm, around some corners and up some hills, lean and rugged Jesse Pomeroy bought "everything that moved and moo'd" from Ed and Elinor Janeway and built it up into a dairy cow operation. He and his then partner managed to get it three-quarters paid off when the partner decided he wanted out. Jesse refinanced and started over.

Elinor, the last of the Janeways, died in 1996, and Barry and Wendy Rowlands bought the farm on the condition that Jesse keep it active. A year or so ago, as he was again about three-quarters paid off, he went through a divorce. Once again he refinanced. "I'm 43 and I've spent the first half of my life working like hell paying off loans and building the business, and I'd like to spend the second half enjoying it more."

So he and his son, Benjamin, and his daughter, Amy, both of whom help on the farm, started poking around for ways to improve the cash flow. They ended up where a good many others have, on Orb Weaver Farm (see chapter 5). As they often do, Marjorie Susman and Marian Pollack made a deep impression on him.

The Pomeroys decided to go into the cheese business. At first, Jesse and Jon Wright at the Taylor Farm were going to build a common cheese house for the two farms, but the idea turned out to be impractical. The Rowlands, however, were so excited about making cheese that they financed the building of a new cheese house. Like the Taylor and Boucher Farms, the new cheese vat is

Marian Pomeroy packs the cheese into molds.

connected directly to the milking line. Enter Peter Dixon, who helped with the design and found the equipment that the Rowlands cheerfully paid for. The vat uses steam instead of hot water to raise the temperature of the milk; the steam is also used to heat the cheese room.

When he first began to build the cheese facility, Jesse didn't want to make his own cheese—so he married Marian, who did. Peter trained Marian, and now Marian and Jesse work together to make a distinctive cheese named after their farm. For the first time since he left the dairy farm in New Hampshire where he was born, he thinks that "we might make a halfway decent living at it."

For 17 years Jesse worked without a vacation, going sometimes a year and a half without even a day off. He's looking forward to cutting the herd down to 30 milkers, half of which will be Jerseys belonging to his daughter. He cuts 150 acres of hay every year from the fields of 15 neighbors who are happy to give it to him. He's found that it's cheaper to buy corn silage than it is to make it, but he won't use the Monsanto-manufactured growth hormone, rBGH: "I have more respect for my cows than that."

In addition to round, plastic-wrapped bales, he also puts up 1,300 square bales for winter. He used to keep his animals in the barn all the time, but he long ago switched to rotational grazing, separating his fields into separate pastures with electric fence and moving the herd to a new grazing area every couple of days.

Now that they are in full operation, Marian spends three days a week making cheese and two days delivering it by hand to various retail food stores and coops in southern and central Vermont. You'll find both Marion and Jesse at the Londonderry Farmer's Market from May through October.

CROWLEY CHEESE COMPANY
Crowley Cheese

The Crowley Cheese Company has been making cheese longer than any other manufacturer in the United States. They have gradually replaced most of the equipment over the years, but since 1882 the cheese has been made in the same building. There is some evidence that it was made and sold out of the Crowley kitchen 20 years before that. In the early days, one of the Crowley sisters opened a beauty parlor on the second floor of the old building. Women bought their cheese on the ground floor and went upstairs to have their hair done. Cindy Dawley, who has been with the company for 13 years, will caution you to watch

Crowley cheese has been made in the same building since 1882.

your step as you climb up the rickety steps into the third-floor attic because the stairs are 119 years old. This is the only cheese facility in the state where you can clearly hear the footsteps of the people working upstairs where the offices and packing facilities are located.

The company was owned and operated by the Crowley family until Robert Crowley died in 1966 at age 56. Ninety-year-old Alfred Crowley, Robert's brother, still lives just up the hill from the weathered old three-story cheese facility. He was for many years the postmaster of Healdville, where the plant is located—in fact, at that time the post office was in his home. Healdville is such a tiny village that until the cheese company began shipping UPS, about two-thirds of the outgoing mail consisted of parcel post cheese for catalog orders.

Randolph Smith, former headmaster of the Little Red Schoolhouse in

New York City, bought the company and made the cheese after Robert Crowley died. His efforts through *Yankee* magazine and other marketing strategies brought Crowley national attention. Unfortunately his cheesemaking career ended abruptly in 1966 when he fell down a couple of low stairs in his home; he died two days later.

The parade of cheesemakers since Randolph Smith died includes a man who was studying to be a mortician. When he passed his boards and left, convinced that death was more profitable than cheese, a woman who had made goat cheese in France took over for about five years. She was replaced by a nice young family man, who was succeeded by Randolph's son, Kent. A couple of years ago Cindy Dawley, the present manager of Crowley, hired Michael Ward, a young bull of a man. He has now been replaced by Jason Huck, a tall, lean young man not long out of high school whose father gave up a successful career in corporate finance to buy an old rundown farm only 5 miles from the Crowley cheese facility.

The Hucks have rebuilt their house and barn and are raising some 65 sheep for meat, along with a few goats. They have also nearly finished a complete cheesemaking facility, but have yet to put it to use. Meanwhile, five days a week Jason is learning his trade just down the road from where he lives.

The Crowley Cheese Company employs only five people. While Mark Brebach handles sales and marketing and helps with the cheesemaking when he has time, the other four work together to make the cheese five days a week.

There are no machines, no conveyor belts, and no pasteurizers. Jason uses wire knives to cut the curd. The only sound in the bright cheese room is the swish of hands through curd and the occasional clink of the rake against the side of the vat as the curds are moved into a parachute-like sieve to remove the whey.

Once the whey has been mostly taken out, Cindy sprays the curd with fresh water while the other three, wearing rubber gloves, keep agitating it with their hands, plunging their arms above their elbows into the warm, soft curds, raking them back and forth, up and down to be sure it all gets thoroughly washed.

Again the liquid is removed and Jason salts the cheese while everyone keeps stirring. After an energetic period of mixing in the salt as thoroughly as possible, Jason packs it into an ancient press that looks as if it has been there since the company began.

At Crowley, no one believes in the new vegetable enzymes or in the biologically engineered microbial rennet derived from fungus. They feel that the traditional use of animal rennet really affects the flavor. (See The Rennet Quandary in the Appendixes.) In the old days, Cindy says, they used to hang a calf's stomach in the basement. When they needed rennet, they soaked the stomach in a bucket of water and poured the water into the warm milk. Result: instant coagulation.

Eight local farms used to supply their milk, but now 30,000 pounds comes into their bulk tank raw and guaranteed rBGH-free every week from two farms in Middlebury.

The whey disposal story is, as usual, both ingenious and time-consuming. The whey is pumped through a pipe, which passes under the road, through some woods, and eventually disgorges into a man-made whey lagoon. In the spring they pump it out and spray it on a 6-acre field nearby.

Plymouth Cheese Company

If Shelburne Farms is the most gorgeous dairy farm in the nation, the President Coolidge State Historic Site in Plymouth is the most serene. Only a mile off Route 100 north, a few old, beautifully maintained white buildings dot an open green carpet of gentle hills with the dark forest rising behind them. It is quiet here. It is so quiet that 40,000 to 50,000 visitors come away from it every year wondering why they feel different.

One of the white buildings is the post office. Another is John Coolidge's home. He is in his mid-90s now, and until a couple of years ago, he owned the site. A third quite sizable building houses the cheese facility that used to produce the venerable Plymouth Cheese, born only a short time after its neighbor, Crowley, came into being.

There isn't a whole lot of difference between the two cheeses. Crowley is a washed-curd sharp Colby, and Plymouth was a granular-curd cheese perhaps a little sweeter than Crowley's because the curd wasn't washed so much. The plant shut down in the 1930s, but John Coolidge reopened it in the 1960s and produced cheese consistently until he sold the site to the state of Vermont in 1998.

One of the conditions of the sale was that Plymouth Cheese continue to be made.

Feeling that cheesemaking was not an appropriate occupation for the state, the department of agriculture asked for proposals from any qualified business that was interested in making Plymouth Cheese on the site. They are still waiting.

Although the last piece of Plymouth Cheese is long gone, the store is open and Mary Earl, who has been there for more than 39 years, is currently selling a variety of Vermont cheeses. And she is waiting patiently for some enterprising and ambitious cheesemaker to become partners with the state of Vermont and restore Plymouth Cheese to its proper place in the pantheon of excellent Vermont cheeses.

Ruth Anne Barker
Chèvre

"I've been doing this for a really long time," says Ruth Anne Barker. "I've done it for . . . ever!" Certainly there is no other farmstead cheesemaker in Vermont who has been making cheese even half as long as Ruth Anne. It all began because she didn't want her children to suffer with asthma the way she has most of her life. She had heard that many children who drink cow's milk and who suffer from allergies and asthma find relief when they switch to goat's milk. So when she finished nursing, she bought a goat for milk to feed her children. Her strategy worked—no asthma. She pawned her engagement ring to buy two more La Mancha goats. "Real nice ring," she says, "amethyst with all these little diamonds."

Ruth Anne loves La Manchas. Her herd name—registered with the American Goat Association—is Revelation La Manchas. She loves them for the flavor of their milk. One goat led to another and ultimately, after many fancy-goat shows, she happened to read a Ph.D. thesis on the technique of cheesemaking in ancient Greece and Turkey. After working for a while at Crowley Cheese, she decided to try it on her own.

She started making cheese in her kitchen and has been doing the same thing for almost a quarter of a century. Like all home cheesemakers she is a fanatic about cleanliness. The health of her herd and her spotless kitchen both testify to that.

On 4 acres of land, she transforms the milk of three La Mancha goats into 20 to 30 pounds of delicious cheese every week from May to October. When she is not making cheese, she is the principal of Leicester Elementary School.

Her husband, Robert, does all the milking and assists at the birthing of the kids, which goat people call "kidding" (but it isn't). He does these things in the small, compact barn he built in 1984 when they moved to their present location a few miles outside Wallingford.

He turns on National Public Radio and, with the help of one of his Corgis, escorts the goats, all of whom have names, to the milking stand, a small platform with a single worn, wooden stanchion on one end. He sits on the platform beside the doe with his bucket. When he ties her right rear leg with a piece of twine to prevent her from capsizing the bucket, she lets her milk down.

When his bucket is full, he takes it into the kitchen and pours it through a sterilized square cloth diaper into a clean glass jar. When Ruth Anne has perhaps 8 gallons in her refrigerator (three or four milkings' worth), she pours it into a stainless-steel container and stirs in ½ pint to 1 pint of culture that she has made herself several days before. Then, if it is spring, she adds 5 drops of rennet to 1 cup of well water and mixes that into the 8 gallons of milk. In the fall, she only needs 2 drops of rennet. This is because animals produce their richest milk near the end of their annual lactation period. Milk that is higher in butterfat requires less coagulant to separate the curds from the whey.

"There's no rule of thumb about any of this," she admits. "It's all pressure, temperature, and what's floating in the air."

She then covers the container and puts a sign on top of it to tell herself when to drain it, usually two days later. After draining the curds she lines a large, cone-shaped colander with two sterilized diapers and puts it in a pasta cooker. The curds and whey go into this and drain for 12 hours.

After that she adds from ¼ to ⅓ cup of ordinary iodized salt, which she mixes in by hand. Now, with all the cheese in the colander, she folds the diaper over the top, holds it tight with a heavy sterling-silver trivet that came to her as a wedding present from a previous marriage, chains a ½-gallon plastic milk container full of water on top, and leaves it alone for another 12 hours. When she finally wraps the cheese in tinfoil, it looks like nothing so much as a giant Hershey's chocolate kiss. She either saves it for the next farmer's market or sells it out the back door to a friend or someone who has called in an order.

There are probably few other graduates of Brown University who can characterize themselves as goat cheesemaker, pianist-vocalist, veterinarian, school principal, de-horner of goats, and massive vegetable gardener. At age 58, Ruth loves where she is and what she is doing.

COBB HILL CHEESE COMPANY
Mount Ascutney; Four Corners Caerphilly

The Cobb Hill Cheese Company in Hartland Four Corners is the first community-operated business of the Cobb Hill Co-Housing Intentional Community being built on an old 250-acre farm. The brainchild of Dartmouth professor Donella Meadows, whose syndicated columns on environmental issues appeared in many local newspapers, the community will eventually be a cluster of 22 families living in 6 duplexes, 7 single homes, and 3 small apartments in a separate common house. More than 14 buildings are nearing completion on a 10-acre piece of sloping land behind the old barn.

Donella Meadows never got to see her dream come true. She died quite suddenly in the winter of 2000, leaving behind her young partners in this revolutionary enterprise, Kerry Gawalt and Stephen Leslie. They met and learned biodynamic farming at the famed Hawthorne Valley Farm in Harlemville, New York, where both were apprenticed. Kerry got there by means of several Waldorf schools. Stephen was raised in southern New Hampshire and had previously spent six years as a

Kerry Gawalt with Cobb Hill Farm's Fjord horses

monk in the Weston Priory after an education in fine arts at the Boston Museum School. Blessed with youth and plenty of farming experience, they have implemented Peter Dixon's business plan and cheese facility design.

They are milking seven cows from their small herd of Jersey and Brown Swiss, and the compact cheese facility is built into the big old 50-stanchion barn, which they have partitioned down to 8. Peter has trained Marsha Carmichael, who has been part of the community since its inception, in the art of making cheese, while Kerry and Stephen concentrate on the animals, the fieldwork, and in summer the enormous 5-acre organic vegetable garden. All of their products, including the cheese, are 100 percent organic.

Marsha is making an Appenzeller type of Swiss cheese, and a Caerphilly-style cheese that she calls Four Corners three times a week in 8- to 12-pound wheels. She ages them a minimum of 3 months but hopes to extend that period to 8 or 10 months soon.

The way the community works, Marsha buys her milk from Stephen and Kerry, who take care of the animals and do the milking. Two young Fjord work-horses, small Norwegian draft horses, do much of the fieldwork using a selection of vintage plows, tillers, and cutters. They also have a gasoline-powered cultivator.

Licensed and certified since July 2000, the Cobb Hill Cheese Company makes its products available at the farm as well as at various Vermont and New Hampshire food coops and health food outlets. The new residents of Cobb Hill are working hard for diversification. Beekeeping, sugaring, orchards, poultry, blueberries, organic vegetables, and cheese are all being initiated by members of the community.

When Donella Meadows finally raised the $600,000 needed to buy the old farm in Hartland Four Corners and put together the last of the private loans and advance payments on the 22 dwellings that at the time existed only on paper, she had no way of knowing that this dream of hers—a cooperative, environmentally friendly, diversified, self-supporting farming enterprise owned and administered by the members of this co-housing community—would become a permanent living memorial to her memory.

THISTLE HILL FARM

To visit Janine and John Putnam is to step back in time into a television episode of *My Three Sons* on a Vermont farm. John doesn't look like Fred MacMurray, but when 12-year-old Ian walks into the kitchen holding a rainbow trout he just pulled from their pond and 14-year-old Lindsey blows through announcing to her lawyer-turned-cheesemaker father that she and her friend are going out for a ride in the woods with Raja and Lark, two of their three horses, you cannot help but feel that you have entered a 21st-century Norman Rockwell painting.

Even the extra-large mudroom looks like a carefully decorated set. All sorts of small and large boots, shoes, socks, hats, and gloves are strewn about its cubby-lined walls, with a Border collie named Chance and a seven-year-old boy named Caleb petting a Corgi named Cordelia in the middle of the casual discards of the day's footwear. The storybook feeling keeps on growing as you learn that there is yet another young boy and a house cat named Hobbes who spends her summers outdoors and probably won't return until fall. There's also an elderly ewe named Lamby, and another cat named Milo with "more toes than you can count." Not to mention the beautifully manicured pond with its rustic sauna, and on and on.

The pigs have their new home not far from the sturdy old barn that John

John and Janine Putnam with one of their herd of 20 Jersey cows

and Janine brought from another farm and reassembled for the 20 Jersey cows that Janine milks. Just up the hill is the cheese facility: a spanking-new building with spacious, airy rooms dominated by a 200-year-old, 850-liter copper kettle.

"You can't make a good Alpine cheese in anything but copper," says Putnam. "You ought to hear what I went through to convince Byron Moyer [the Vermont dairy inspector] to let me use this great old kettle that I brought over from Switzerland."

The facility has what John calls "up the air drainage," which simply means that all the stinky places on the farm are downwind and won't contaminate the cheese. He refers offhandedly to his hard-won equipment, most of it bought in Europe, as merely "a hammer in a carpenter's hand," which places him in full agreement with all the other Vermont farmstead cheesemakers.

How did this Middlebury College and Vermont Law School graduate, who still practices law part time in Hanover, New Hampshire, end up making organic Alpine-style cheese in the hills of the quaintly English township of North Pomfret, Vermont? Perhaps the story began with his father's love of good smelly goat cheese. John, who is in his mid-40s, has lived in Vermont since he was 10. He met and married Janine at Vermont Law School, where she was studying environmental law. After graduation, John got a job with a Boston firm specializing in U.S. labor law.

"I had half a day off in the first month," he says. "It was a Sunday afternoon and I looked around at all of these successful people and had no trouble deciding that I didn't want to spend the best part of my life trying to get where they were." So he and Janine bought Thistle Hill Farm and over the past 17 years have added all the children and animals described above. They expect to be in full operation and making an aged cows' milk cheese similar to Beaufort by May 2002.

These are people who enjoy challenges; making a cheese that John feels is not being made well in this country is the most recent challenge. "If you have ever ridden a bike in the woods fast and well," he says, "you know that the goal is to go one gear faster." While he still enjoys pleading cases before the Vermont Supreme Court, some of which involve well over a million dollars, he finds cheesemaking "many gears faster" than anything he has done so far.

KAREN BIXLER
Aged Raclette

When I first visited Karen Bixler at her farm in Bethel, I thought I had made a wrong turn and ended up at one of those legendary abandoned Vermont farms with its falling-down house nearly buried in the overgrown hay. Only the old Toyota pickup and the barking of many dogs announced the presence of human life. Since that time, however, her goats and Gratitude, her Jersey calf, have cleaned up the yard, and she has hung some flowers from the balcony. She may even have the house painted one of these days.

Karen, a woman in her 50s, lives here alone, if you call living with Casper the cat, Carmella Sunday the Jersey cow, her calf, three dogs, two healthy pigs, and a passel of goats being alone. She bought this 10-acre piece of land 8 years ago after returning from Europe, where she had resided for the 22 years before that.

During her summers there, she lived in the high Alps near the French border. It was there that she learned to make Raclette. In the incredibly steep country above the tree line, cheesemaking was necessarily primitive but amazingly effective. To dissipate any glamour his students might attach to cheesemaking, her "Kasemeister" used to hammer them with the three equally important parts of creating a good cheese: the kessey (the pot used to make the cheese), the cellar where the cheese is aged, and the washup. To slight any one of them was to court disaster.

Born in Westchester County, New York, Karen has a son in Switzerland, one brother in Connecticut, and several more in California. When she returned to this country nine years ago, she went to work for Bunny and Peter Flint at The Organic Cow, which at the time was making some of the most interesting farmstead cheese in the state. But the yen to make her own cheese the way she had learned to do it in Switzerland would occasionally overpower her. From time to time, she would pick up a few gallons of milk from a neighbor and create her own Raclette, which she sold out of her house. People liked it so much that she decided to buy a cow for motivational purposes. Cows have to be milked, and the milk needs to be used right away. The pigs arrived to put the whey to use.

Karen and Casper love to have visitors. If the day is warm, she will serve you some of her cheese on homemade bread with a cup of tea and talk about how she wishes that she could sell her cheese in the local markets, and how she would love to put up a signboard the size of her barn saying that she is proud not to be FDA inspected. "I think that would be the best advertising I could have."

She loves to show off her tiny, cluttered kitchen, where she makes her cheese on the woodstove. "To me, it's a very meditative process," she says, explaining that she got used to a woodstove in Switzerland and really prefers it. "I love that it's such an ancient craft."

If you ask, she will happily show you her low-ceilinged, gravel-floored, natural-stone-walled basement, where hanging from rafters are handmade shelves on which her cheeses are curing. One of them, given to her by a friend, has slots cut in it so that the wheels may be cured standing up. She turns and brushes each of them almost every day.

"I guarantee my cheese," she says. "If you get a bad wheel, I'll replace it at no cost."

She loves the independence of cheesemaking and would someday like to make a goat's milk Camembert. This is farmstead cheesemaking in its most basic form, and Karen Bixler, like Ruth Ann Barker, is 100 percent committed to her work.

"I have a good butcher, a good inseminator, and a good plumber," she says. "I'll never move."

Neighborly Farms
Organic Homestead Flavored Cheddars; Feta; Colby; Muenster; Provolone

"I was born in this house and I'm going to die in it," says Robert Dimmick, co-owner (with his wife, Linda) of Neighborly Farms in North Randolph. The

Robert Dimmick with his daughter outside their cheese facility and retail store.

name originated when he took over the dairy farm from his father and converted the 240-foot barn from a free-stall into a stanchion arrangement. While the reconstruction was going on, he rented a neighbor's empty barn for his milking herd. Thus was Neighborly Farms born.

Snugly tucked into a newly painted and renovated white farmhouse with three dormer windows looking out unblinkingly on the nearly flat open fields that surround the house and barn, Robert and Linda, in their mid-30s, are cozily tucked in with Robert's parents and his older brother and sister, all of whom have homes on the same large acreage. The buildings of Neighborly Farms are distributed on three of the four corners of an intersection of dirt roads: the house on one, the barn diagonally across from it, and Robert's shop on the third.

After raising and home schooling three stepping-stone children, Bobby, Bailey, and Billy, aged 8, 9, and 10 respectively, the Dimmicks decided it was time to stop fighting the losing battle of keeping a 48-cow family dairy farm financially solvent. Their solution was cheese.

They made a painless transition to organic farming methods and became the most recent and one of the most ambitious farmstead cheesemakers in the state. Their preparations were intense and well thought out. To learn about making cheese they visited several ongoing operations and brought in the ever-helpful Peter Dixon (see chapter 3). The three of them spent several hardworking days in their kitchen making several different kinds of cheese.

They contacted State Dairy Inspector Greg Lockwood early and frequently as they built the large, bright cheese room and aging facility that is nested inside the front end of the barn, a new building inside an old building. Their two cheese vats came from Qualtech, a Quebec company specializing in small cheesemaking equipment. In a separate refrigerated room there is a sizable bulk tank with a built-in agitator to use for brining the cheeses. They went to a great deal of trouble and expense to put a special surface coating on all the rooms to make them easier to clean. They have even installed some movable wall sections in case they ever need to move large equipment around.

The Dimmicks are plungers. They decided early on to go for broke and to convert all the milk from their Holstein herd into making as many as six or seven different cheeses. They began with a mild, creamy Cheddar and then began adding flavors. Their list now includes garlic, chili, salsa, hot pepper, green onion, and sage, with more on the way. They are also making a mild Feta, a Mozzarella, and have plans for Provolone. ("We want to make a gift-style Provolone," says Linda, "with the string wrapped around it so you can hang it from the ceiling the way they did in the old Italian cheese stores.") Finally, they would love to make an organic orange-rind Muenster. ("I grew up on Muenster," says Robert, "so I'm making that for my own sake.")

This is for the most part a do-it-yourself operation. They have built a special room with a loading dock for packaging and distributing their own products. They sell all their cheeses, as well as several other Vermont products, from a small, attractive store in front of the cheese room. Curious visitors can move from the store down a hallway lined on both sides by picture windows. On one side they can watch Linda making cheese; on the other they can look into the main barn area where Rob is tending the calves and the milking cows.

With working family dairy farms becoming almost legendary, the Dimmicks, along with several other Vermont cheesemakers, have expanded their facilities into full-scale tourist attractions and are looking forward to being included on the itineraries of the tour buses that come up from New York City and Boston. Visitors can taste the fresh warm curd as it comes out of the vats, as well as all of their finished products, while their children play with one or more of Bailey's eight cats or the young Australian shepherd farm dog.

In contrast to other larger companies that make only a few organic Cheddars, Neighborly Farms has moved lock, stock, and cheese barrel into 100 percent new age organic dairy farming.

VERMONT BUTTER AND CHEESE COMPANY
Goat Fontina; Goat Feta; Bonne Bouche; Chèvre; Herb Chèvre; Pepper Chèvre; Chèvrier; Impastata; Fromage Blanc; Crème Fraîche; Mascarpone

If Vermont Shepherd is the flagship of the cheese movement in this state, Allison Hooper, cofounder of the Vermont Butter and Cheese Company, is the power behind its remarkable growth. She is the principal motivating force, problem solver, and, if there is such a thing, unofficial leader.

Sparked by a remark that Rich Chalmers, her marketing director, dropped about what the small vineyards in northern California had done for themselves by banding together, she singlehandedly created the Vermont Cheese Council, a primary glue that holds the farmstead cheese movement together.

Its precursor was another of her ideas: a Vermont Cheese Festival featuring all the Vermont-made cheeses that was held in spring 1996 on the occasion of Vermont Butter and Cheese Company being awarded the Vermont Small Business of the year award. Everybody who was anybody in Vermont, including Governor Howard Dean, came to make speeches, Shelburne Farms hosted the event, and Allison arranged for its extensive promotion. Its success catapulted Vermont cheese to national importance.

Allison's real life began at age 18 when as a college French major she spent a semester in Paris and did not want to return. She landed a summer job on a farm in Brittany that made a Tomme de Savoie sort of cheese from the milk of 12 Jersey cows. The milk from their 40 goats went into a variety of chèvres, and she also learned to appreciate the fresh butter, crème fraîche, and fromage blanc they made and sold at the local farmer's markets. That summer job worked out so well that after graduation Allison returned to France to work on a goat farm.

She loved the life in the French countryside. She remembers watching all the goats from the various farms flood the streets after morning milking on their way to graze the surrounding hillsides. Then, at night, each family took its bell to the edge of the village to call them back in. They cooled the evening milk in a common cistern. In the morning they added the warm new milk to the cool old milk, stirred in some rennet, and made cheese. The only culture they used was whey from the previous day's milking.

On her return to this country, Allison moved to Vermont because it was a dairy state and because she had a strong connection to her late grandmother's home in Barnard. A farm extension agent in Middlebury sent her to the only goat dairy in the state, the Hooper Farm in Brookfield. She landed an internship, which eventually led to her marriage to one of the Hoopers eight years later.

As an intern at the farm, she also worked in the dairy lab at the state department of agriculture. Bob Reese, who was in charge of marketing there, was organizing the "Taste of Vermont," an award event to honor the Vermont chef who used the most Vermont products. The host of the event was Chef Anton Flore at the Topnotch Restaurant in Stowe. He wanted to use goat cheese, but there was none being made in Vermont at the time. Bob knew about Allison's background and asked her if she would be willing to make some goat cheese for Chef Flore. She did, and at the awards dinner several of the participating chefs asked her to make some for them, too. So she and Bob formed the partnership that became Vermont Butter and Cheese Company.

They converted the milk house at the Hooper Farm into a cheese room. Allison worked seven days a week making crème fraîche and fromage blanc in addition to the chèvres, while Bob sold everything out of the back of his Subaru. Julia Child had just introduced the country to crème fraîche and fromage blanc, and the demand soared. The Hooper Farm boosted the new venture by letting Bob and Allison take over the bottled milk business and make cheese.

At those rare times that she could get away from the cheese room, Allison prowled New York City restaurants convincing the chefs that they should use her products. She looks back a little ruefully at those crazy days: Today she wouldn't dare sell the cheeses she made then.

From the start, she made the cheese and Bob handled the business. By 1987 the demand for their cheese was more than the converted milk house could handle. They moved to the present location, a large warehouselike metal building in an industrial park not far from the famous Websterville Granite Quarries. They now employ 17 people and have a contract with a milk truck to pick up goat's milk from 21 producers. In order to maintain a consistent high quality, Vermont Butter pays these producers a special premium.

Because they had to show a profit from the beginning, they could only afford to make fresh cheese. Waiting for an aged cheese to mature would ruin them. Twelve years went by before they dared to develop the Goat Fontina and the Chèvrier.

In 1990, at the suggestion of a New York distributor, they became the first in this country to make Mascarpone. But Feta looked all but impossible. There was no way they could produce a pure goat Feta that would compete with all the low-priced cow's milk Feta on the market. That's when Don LaRose appeared. When he joined the company five years ago, he brought with him the solution to the Feta problem. After 22 years making cheese for Stella Foods in Hinesburg, Vermont, where he became production manager, he knew how to make good Feta at a reasonable cost.

At Stella he learned a great deal about making cheese from Mauritz Keller, a visiting cheesemaker from Switzerland, and returned the favor by teaching Mauritz to speak English. Apart from Don, the other Stella cheesemakers were licensed by the state of Wisconsin. Vermont does not require a license, but Don wanted to have one. So he called the University of Wisconsin and asked if he could take their final exam without attending the course. Rather reluctantly, they agreed. He flew to Wisconsin, easily passed the test, and today is the only licensed cheesemaker in Vermont.

A native Vermonter who has lived all his life in Bristol, Don is a family man who loves his job. At work he moves easily through every department, assisting each operation as needed. At any given moment you'll find him putting boxes of cheese on a conveyor belt in the shipping room, or checking the frozen culture, or monitoring every step of the Feta and Fontina operations, checking the state of the curd in the time-honored way of putting his hand in it and raising it slowly, watching closely for that magic moment when it cracks over his thumb, the exact right time for cutting.

He has learned a great deal from Allison and is grateful to be able to discuss problems with someone who speaks his language—who knows what pH means and when the moisture is right. He has also studied with Paul Kindstedt at the University of Vermont. Among other things, Professor Paul taught him how to age cheese. Don calls his Goat Fontina a "fussy cheese" because of the care that must be lavished on it during its three months of aging.

CABOT CREAMERY
Cabot Provate Stock; Cabot Vintage Cheddar; Cabot Extra Sharp Cheddar; Cabot Light Cheddar

The men responsible for Vermont's oldest and best-known Cheddar cheeses were both hired by their respective companies right out of high school. After 30 years neither has ever worked anywhere else. They are Scott Fletcher of Grafton Village Cheese Company (see chapter 3) and Marcel Gravel of Cabot Creamery. Cabot Creamery began in 1919 when 94 local dairy farmers each contributed five dollars per cow and a cord of wood to fuel the boiler and bought their first cheese plant.

Marcel, the present plant manager at Cabot, is a young-looking grandfather. Like Scott, he is largely self-taught. Aside from seminars at Utah State and Cornell University, he learned his craft the hard way by working in all phases of its manufacture. He still talks about the time in his early days at the Cabot Creamery when the company installed an entirely new line of equipment. The problem was that no one knew how to operate it, and several weeks of round-the-clock work went by before they learned. Then he moved to the waxing room and the cheese floor, where he learned "flipping, ditching, milling, and salting the curd," up to the finishing table, where he discovered pH and proper acidity. This was followed by nine years as cheese cook, when he was in charge of maintaining constant temperatures at every stage of the process.

After all these years, Marcel still loves his work and remains involved with all of its operations. "There's an art to making cheese. A little more to it than just reading it out a book if you want to make a good-quality product," he says with conviction. "If you want to get the most you can out of that pound of milk."

He's proud of Cabot and especially proud of the people who work there. Proud of the fact that the man in charge of quality control, the cheese taster, has been there for nearly 40 years; the manager of the cottage cheese department for almost 27 years; the supervisor in the cheese room for 22; and a couple of women in the office for 40. He's proud of the awards Cabot has won, particularly those from the "old-timers" at the Wisconsin Cheese Makers Association.

He's proud of making 99.45 percent of all Cabot cheese in his plant, although Cabot has two other plants in Vermont and one in Massachusetts. And he's proud of what he calls his "starter program, the heart of making cheese." This fully automated process, which manufactures all the cultures used in Cabot's many cheeses, takes 15 to 16 hours in the company's own lab. He's proud of the plant's preventive maintenance program, which has virtually eliminated any downtime. And he's proud of turning more than half a million pounds of milk a day into good cheese.

The Cabot workday begins at 1 A.M. when a cheesemaker arrives. After sanitizing all the equipment, he fills the 32,000-pound vats with milk, adds the culture and the enzyme, lets it coagulate for about 28 minutes, cuts it three ways, and, after 3 to 5 minutes in the whey, begins a gentle agitation. The curd is then transferred to the finishing table, where the whey is drained off and the cheddaring done.

After milling, a vacuum pump sucks up the curd and disgorges it into the top of the famous Cabot tower, a 60-foot-high cylinder that is under a heavy vacuum. As the column is filled, it is lowered a little at a time to allow a guillotine blade to slice off a block, which is immediately subjected to a 30-second "pressing cycle" at 100 pounds per square inch. It is then slipped into a vacuum pack, sealed, and dropped out the bottom onto a conveyor belt. The whole process takes 20 minutes from the time the curd goes in at the top to the moment a 42-pound block, wrapped and sealed, drops out at the bottom.

Marcel feels that despite Cabot's automation, the farmer is still a major part of the process. He says that over the past few decades the quality of the milk has improved enormously. Even the milk truck drivers have become more conscientious and thorough. They keep careful records and take samples from each farm. "Making cheese is a team effort all the way through from the farmer to the cheesemaker."

THREE OWLS DAIRY
Red Waxed Paisan Cheese; Natural Rind Paisan Cheese

Vermont Route 100 out of Ludlow winds north through a narrow valley; past a former dairy farm whose fields are now filled with used cars; over an iron bridge into Rochester, and finally into Granville. There, right on the highway, at the first farm past the town clerk's office, you will find Dan Hewitt's herd of sheep guarded by an ever-alert llama. Dan is a timber framer and furniture maker who was born and brought up in England. His wife, Hilary, is American born but grew up overseas.

After Dan got his Ph.D. in animal genetics, the couple decided to move

Dan herds his flock of East Friesian and Dorset sheep with the help of Curtis, a young visitor from New York

back to this country because there weren't enough trees in England. While driving from a friend's house in Maine to investigate California, they drove through Vermont. Once through the state, they stopped, looked at each other, turned around, and drove back. They never reached California.

Next to the big white barn in Granville, you will see a tiny portable milk-

Emily Hewitt feeds one of the flock.

ing parlor sitting in the field next to Dan's flock of East Friesian and Dorset sheep. It consists of two stanchions built into a small horse trailer, with a chute leading up to it on one side and an exit on the other. Dan has started small, milking no more than 20 ewes. He says this gives him plenty of milk to do what he wants to do. "I've always wanted to have sheep, but it's not practical to have sheep except as a way to burn money," he says, "unless you can do something with them."

Dan doesn't live on the farm. Nor does he make cheese there. He and his wife and two children, Sam, eight, and Emily, six, live in a modern post-and-beam chalet that he built himself on a hill a mile or two away. In the basement, which is actually the ground floor of the house, is a complete cheese facility. Bright and airy and extremely compact, it contains all the equipment Dan needs to make the Paisan, or peasant cheese he started with. He hopes someday to make Brin d'Amour, the great Basque cheese from Corsica.

He is marketing his cheeses at the Mad River Valley Farmer's Market in Waitsfield and plans to build a roadside stand at the farm in Granville to sell them and homegrown vegetables. "I like the farmer's market," he says in his pleasant English accent. "You can get direct feedback there because you meet the same people every week."

As an animal geneticist Dan looks forward to breeding the East Friesians with some of the more primitive breeds for a healthy, hardy, and productive herd. He's strong and young and hardworking and has always wanted to raise his children in the country where they could take part in the family business if they wanted to.

As you stand beside Route 100 in Granville and watch a man, his two children, and his llama gather the sheep for the evening milking on a bright summer day, you can see that he has definitely accomplished the first part of his life plan.

Three Shepherds of the Mad River Valley
Vermont Brabander; Aurora

Fourteen-year-old Jackie Faillace is the youngest cheesemaker in the United States. With a little help from her father, she makes all of their cheeses. A born cook, Jackie has been cooking entire meals for the family since she was nine. When they first started, her sister, Heather, 15, used to milk their 35 purebred East Friesian ewes. Like Dan Hewitt at Three Owls Dairy, she milked them in the field on a custom-made rolling milking parlor. Instead of bringing the sheep in for milking twice a day, they pulled the parlor into the pasture in which the sheep were grazing. Her older brother, Francis, 17, was in charge of the fields.

Jackie and Linda Faillace serve cheese to a visitor

Her father, Larry, originally a New Jersey boy, met her mother, Linda, while getting his Ph.D. in animal science at Virginia Tech. Later, during a post-doctoral stint at the University of Nottingham in England, they decided they had to do something in agriculture together—something that would involve their children, be enjoyable, and be financially sound. The whole family was in on the decision to raise sheep and make cheese.

Linda and Larry visited 26 different cheesemakers in five different countries. They then brought in Freddy Michiels, a Belgian cheesemaker, to help them get started. He showed them how to make 14 standard cheeses. After attending a number of seminars and taking some short, intensive college courses, Jackie, then only 12 years old, developed the cheeses she now makes.

They built a bright, airy cheese facility on a 92-acre piece of land on a high, level plateau above Warren, Vermont. This land is managed by a nonprofit corporation called Rootswork, a conglomeration of many community members who all believe in sustainable agriculture. Rootswork maintains a 1-acre organic garden right outside the cheese room. Last summer, the Faillaces built a cave next to the cheese room. They made it out of bales of straw plastered inside and out and sunk a short distance below ground level to ensure good drainage. There is no refrigeration inside. A circulating fan and a damp floor, together with the breathable walls, keep the temperature and humidity inside constant year-round.

Jackie gets cow's milk for the Aurora and the Brabander she makes from the neighboring Von Trapp farm (run by the son and daughter of one of the original Von Trapps of *Sound of Music* fame, who settled in the Mad River Valley after World War II). When Jackie's cheese becomes fully mature, Heather and Linda move it out of the cave into a former one-room schoolhouse located only a few steps away. There, mother and daughter run the charming country store that the former school has been turned into. Heather sells her sister's cheeses, among other things, to local residents and passing tourists.

Jackie, her father, and Freddie Michiels also give summer workshops in cheesemaking to adults from all over the country. An exceptionally bright student, Jackie has already been flagged by Johns Hopkins University to become a member of the class of 2009. With all the Faillaces deeply involved in this enterprise, this is one family business that earns its name in the most literal sense of the word.

Except that it's not quite what they had in mind. For one thing, there are no longer any sheep on the farm. In the summer of 2000, Larry and Linda were called into the Vermont office of the USDA and told that their sheep had tested positive for TSE (transmissible spongiform encephalopathy) and might even be carrying its most virulent form, bovine spongiform encephalopathy, or BSE, the dreaded mad cow disease that recently swept through England for the second time in five years. The USDA offered to buy the Faillace's East Friesian sheep at market prices, after which they would be destroyed in order to eliminate any possibility of the disease getting into this country.

According to Linda Detwiler, senior staff veterinarian for the USDA and a 15-year specialist in TSE and its related forms, "The disease is too devastating to take chances."

Claiming shoddy science and inconclusive evidence, Larry Faillace and Houghton Freeman, owner of Skunk Hollow Farm, the only other farm with a herd of East Friesian sheep imported from Belgium, decided to resist the USDA and refused to sell their sheep.

This produced a pitched battle with intercontinental repercussions that reads like a bad novel, spawning headlines such as "Small Farmers Crushed by

Big Government" and "United States Threatened by Mad Cow Disease"—depending on which side of the controversy you believe. Even the Vermont Cheese Council, usually a model of solidarity for its members, has been shattered by this event, some applauding the Faillaces and the Freeman Foundation for their courage, others quietly advising them to give it up and let it blow over before it ruins Vermont's rapidly expanding farmstead cheese industry.

The situation became so volatile that even though there is no evidence anywhere in the world of mad cow disease being transferred to humans from milk products, Dr. Jan Carney, Vermont's commissioner of health, issued a public warning not to eat Vermont cheese, especially cheese made on those two farms.

There were reams of testimony from experts flown into Vermont from England and the Midwest, court hearings before impartial judges, community demonstrations of support for the Faillaces, a midwinter citizens protest at the Vermont State House in Montpelier, and several last-minute court appeals. There was even an offer from the Belgian government to buy the sheep back, but it was turned down by the USDA, even though Mr. Freeman agreed to pay for the cost of transport. There was a new but still inconclusive test called the Western Blot, and petitions to save the animals were circulated in Vermont. Despite all this, the sheep were picked up by government trucks in February 2001 and held for further testing on government property.

Meanwhile, Jackie the cheesemaker has been making cow cheese. "What we'd really like to do," says Heather plaintively, "is get more sheep." The best they can hope for until the USDA pays them for their confiscated herd is to buy sheep's milk from a neighbor and get on with their lives.

SHELBURNE FARMS
Vermont Farmhouse Cheddar; Extra Aged Cheddar

Nowhere in the United States is there a more beautiful dairy farm in a more spectacular setting. Fourteen hundred acres of intensely green fields sloping gently down to the blue waters of Lake Champlain are home to magnificently restored Tudor-style farm buildings and a herd of purebred Brown Swiss cattle housed in what is certainly the world's most luxurious barn. Though not privately owned, this is a working farm, a great part of whose revenue comes from the thousands of tourists who are attracted to its turn-of-the-20th-century opulence.

Originally built in 1880 by Dr. William Seward and Lila Vanderbilt Webb as an experiment to demonstrate new techniques and practices in land use and farming, today Shelburne Farms operates as a nonprofit environmental educa- tion center. It is supported by membership and visitor fees, as well as by the proceeds from the 24-room Inn at Shelburne Farms, the Seward's former home; a bakery; a large organic garden; a furniture-making shop; and the internation- ally renowned cheesemaking facility.

Jamie Miller, a tall young cheesemaker who replaced Ross Gagnon about a year ago, presides over Shelburne Farms' sparkling-clean, state-of-the-art cheese- making facility. He grew up in Lancaster County, Pennsylvania, and graduated

The Norman-style barn at Shelburne Farms is one of the largest farm buildings in the country.

from New England Culinary Institute, cutting his chef's teeth in its many fine restaurants.

Shelburne Farms has been making cheese since 1980. Jamie, only the third cheesemaker since the plant's inception, does not use animal rennet. He is having good luck with a chemically synthesized coagulant. In addition to the regular sharp Cheddar, he is making some three-year-old and even some five-year-old cheese, all of which is being aged on the premises. He makes cheese to the tune of a Bach cantata, and his approach is also classic and very much hands-on. He firmly believes that touch is his most important sense. He wants to know at all times what the cheese feels like.

In answer to a tourist's classic question, "How come you don't make anything else but Cheddar?" he answers: "Well, when we get it right I guess we'll try something else."

Marjorie Susman and Marian Pollack of Orb Weaver in front of their cheese cave.

CHAPTER 5

The Cheesemakers of Northwestern Vermont

ORB WEAVER FARM

Vermont Farmhouse Cheese; Cave Aged Farmhouse Cheese

Fresh out of agricultural school in Massachusetts, two young women, Marjorie Susman and Marian Pollack, wanted desperately to work on a farm. When they were offered the job of running a dairy farm in New Haven, Vermont, they leaped at the chance, cheerfully ignoring the fact that the house was falling down and the barn was in the final stages of decay.

Ever since she can remember, Marian has wanted to make cheese. She pestered her parents at home, her teachers at elementary school, her professors in college, and finally her new landlords in New Haven. Swayed by her enthusiasm, the owners took out a second mortgage on the farm to finance construction of a cheese room, while Marian began to read everything she could lay her hands on about how to make farmstead cheese. And as if that weren't enough, fledgling farmers Marian and Marjorie also found time to put in a 4-acre organic vegetable garden.

In the beginning, it was an uphill battle. Gradually, they rebuilt the buildings. Twice a day in a barn without a gutter cleaner, they milked 30 cows and made cheese. Seven or eight local restaurants bought all the vegetables they grew. Then, one fine summer evening, they looked blearily at each other and wondered what in the world they were doing to themselves and why.

They stopped making cheese for two and a half years. Despite the fact that the quality of their milk was judged to be third best in Vermont for the size of the herd, they decided to sell most of the cows, leaving just enough of their beloved Jerseys to make cheese twice a week. What they expected to be a difficult sale proved to be quick and easy. A good farmer only 5 miles away bought the whole group. To this day, they drive over to visit "the girls" whenever they feel the urge. Six cows are not enough to heat the barn in winter, so Marjorie and Marian buy back all their heifers from the same farmer every year and take care of them through the cold weather. Then they sell them to him again in the spring.

By making 3 tons of cheese from these six Jersey cows in the winter, and by selling their beautiful organic vegetables in the summer to the same places that have bought them for the past 18 years, they have balanced their workloads so

that they can do what they love to
do when they want to do it and still
pay the bills. Most important, they
now have time to watch the sunsets
and putter in the flower garden.
They're still workaholics, but they're
working at what they most enjoy.

Playing CDs of classical music,
Marian does the milking. They col-
laborate on making the cheese and
cultivating the garden. Their cozy
cheese room is dug into the side of
a hill just a stone's throw from the
bright and airy barn. Not far from

Inside the cheese cave at Orb Weaver

there, they have recently dug a cave into the side of the hill that they now use
for curing all their cheese. From the outside it has an almost prehistoric Celtic
look about it.

When Marjorie and Marian first began to make cheese, people asked what
kind it was and where they had learned how to do it. The only formal education
they had in cheesemaking was a one-day workshop they had taken 20 years ago.
Then they experimented in the kitchen, making their own culture, until they
came up with one they liked (they now buy the culture because the results are

far more consistent). So in order to answer the first of these questions, they had to scurry over to their cheese books. After scanning the descriptions of various common kinds of cheese in their how-to books, they decided that Colby came the closest to describing what they were making.

Situated on the rim of a wide bowl of farmland bordered by timber, perhaps 20 miles in diameter, Orb Weaver Farm started with only 28 acres. They have now managed to buy more acreage and are seriously considering growing their own hay. The worst day of their lives happened a few years ago. Marjorie, a fanatic about using good feed for her Jersey cows, couldn't locate any that satisfied her and settled for a truckload of second-cut alfalfa from Colorado. When the truck arrived, it turned out that the bales weighed 150 pounds each, and the truck got stuck trying to reach their barn.

A neighbor interrupted his fieldwork to bring his tractor over and pull the truck out while several friends arrived to help with the huge bales. On top of the load, Marjorie pulled too hard on one of them; when it suddenly gave way she went plunging to the ground far below. "I could hear the scream clear up in the loft," said Marian. (Aside from some colorful bruises and a lot of difficulty doing the milking for a couple of weeks, Marjorie was miraculously unhurt.) Then, in the middle of the unloading, it began to rain and the truck got stuck a second time trying to get out. The same neighbor returned with two tractors to pull it out a second time.

To put the icing on the cake, when Marjorie fed the new alfalfa out, none of the cows would eat it. They backed away in horror because it was so violently green. Marjorie had to mix it with some drab old Vermont hay before they would touch it.

Every part of this efficient little farm feeds every other part. Whey from the cheese feeds the pastures, manure from the cows feeds the garden, and the vegetables from the garden feed Marjorie and Marian.

WILLOW HILL FARM
Autumn Oak; Alder Brook; Cobble Hill; Summertomme; Mountain Tomme; Fernwood

Right next to Cindy Major's picture in her 11th-grade yearbook is the photo of another dark-haired girl named Willow Smart. The two didn't know each other at the time, but a couple of years ago Willow ended up making Vermont Shepherd cheese with Cindy. She now produces and sells three or four of her own cheeses to restaurants in New York, Washington, D.C., and Boston, in addition to farmer's markets, stores, by mail order, and at Willow Hill Farm where she makes them.

Willow Hill wasn't much of a farm when she and her husband, Dave Phinney, bought it in 1991. It became even less of a farm in 1996 when the only building on it, the barn, burned down. Fortunately it was empty. They had made the decision to apprentice at Major Farm, and had just built and moved into a garage with an overhead apartment. They rebuilt the barn on its original

Willow Smart and Dave Phinney in front of the cave at Willow Hill

foundation, but redesigned it for milking sheep and making cheese. This allowed plenty of room for the milking parlor, well separated from the cheese room to assure that no barn air would get into the cheesemaking area.

By this time they had replaced most of the goldenrod, the only vegetation on this bleak piece of land when they bought it. They planted a large pick-it-yourself berry patch and erected two greenhouses for growing herbs and bedding plants for commercial nurseries. All their products are organically grown.

Halfway up the mile-long driveway that leads to their home, Dave and Willow have recently built a sizable cave for aging their cheeses. Dave dug it out of the side of Willow Hill; its back wall is actually the rock ledge of the hill itself. A trickle of underground water runs down its face into a cement drain he has installed as part of the foundation. This keeps the cave at a nearly constant high humidity, while the thick layer of earth on top maintains a steady temperature of 52 to 56 degrees. Power for lights and fans comes from a nearby solar panel. The outside is beautifully landscaped into a small woodsy park where you can sit and listen to the birds sing. Or swat mosquitoes, whichever is appropriate.

Dave does the milking and takes care of the animals, while four times a week Willow makes all the cheese and tends to the aging process. Last year they milked 33 ewes from their mixed flock of purebred Friesians, Dorset Friesian crosses, Suffolk Friesian crosses, and purebred Dorsets. Willow believes that a flock like this has a lot of "hybrid vigor," and she backs up that belief by pointing out that she gets an average of 1 pound of cheese for each 4 pounds of milk for the whole May through October milking season.

Willow is still amazed that she, who was born in Hawaii, ended up marrying a man who was brought up not 5 miles from where they have bought this old abandoned farm, not because it was near his place of birth but because it was the only farm in the whole state they could afford.

Then consider those two girls who didn't know each other when their pictures were put side by side in their 11th-grade high school yearbook, but who would end up years later working side by side again with their hands in the same vat making sheep cheese. Coincidence or part of a grand plan? Your choice.

Does' Leap Farm
Fresh Chèvre

Here's another farm cut out of the wilderness by the young couple who live on it. As you drive south on Route 108 out of Bakersfield, you can't see any sign of it except an old mailbox with one long name and one short name on it. A deserted dirt road wanders up the hill into some scrub growth.

You wouldn't know it, but this is one of the pastures for a herd of Nubian and Alpine mixed-breed goats that a city boy and a country girl have put together in order to produce milk for six excellent cheeses. George Van Vlaanderen from New York City and Kristan Doolan, a native Vermonter whose family still lives in nearby Fletcher, met at the University of Vermont and went on together to a graduate course at the University of Maine, where they dreamed of starting a dairy.

"How about goats?" asked Kristan.

"Fine," answered George.

They were lucky to find their 130 acres of virgin land not far from Kristan's parents and close enough to Burlington to use it as a market for their products.

They brought in a portable sawmill and cut enough timber to build a couple of sheds, pens, and a cheese facility with a second story in which they could live until such time as they could build a real house. Stocking the pens with a few goats, they attended Paul Kindstedt's classes at the University of Vermont and several workshops with Peter Dixon. Kristan began a year of stovetop experimentation to develop various cheeses while George made hundreds of phone calls to find small, inexpensive equipment that could pass the rigorous standards of the Vermont Department of Agriculture. Their cheese vat, for example, doubles as a pasteurizer and was originally a culinary steam kettle for making large quantities of soup in a restaurant. They heat this and the living quarters upstairs with an outdoor wood furnace, much like the Boucher Farm up the road (see page 104).

Kristan and George credit the superior quality of their organic cheeses to what Kristan calls rotational brush grazing. Goats are natural browsers, she says, so rather than eat grass, which tends to be loaded with parasites, their goats browse through a mixture of grass and scrub growth in the surrounding young forest. Instead of fenced pastures, they have fenced woodlots, separated into many small browsing plots by movable electric fence. Using a system of rotational grazing, they and their Border collie, Max, move the animals from one to another as the browse is depleted. Eating the leaves of the scrub growth along with the grass and herbs growing under it produces a milk of unusually high quality and imparts a unique flavor to the cheese.

Two or three of Burlington's best restaurants snap up a good part of the cheese they make; the rest they sell at the farmer's market. The Cheese Trader, a local gourmet wine and cheese shop, takes whatever is left over. With their goats, their pigs, their chickens, their large organic garden, and their three-year-old child, they qualify 100 percent as one of the few fully organic farmstead goat cheesemakers in the United States. (See also The Lazy Lady in chapter 6.)

GREEN MOUNTAIN BLUE CHEESE
Vermont Blue Cheese; Gore-Dawn-Zola

Dawn Morin-Boucher and her husband, Daniel, are young, state-of-the-art cheesemakers and farmers. The Boucher family has been dairy farming for 12 generations, 9 in Canada and 3 in their present location in the northwest corner of Vermont near Highgate Center. When Daniel's father inherited the farm, *his* father was milking 14 cows. Now Daniel and his brother do all the work of milking and caring for 160 Holsteins plus equally as many young stock.

Diminutive Dawn met Daniel on a blind date set up by a teammate on the local softball team who happened to be married to Daniel's brother. Fourteen months later, on Valentine's Day, they married and settled on Daniel's family farm. Dawn was convinced that what the 800-acre farm needed was value-added products to make them less dependent on the vagaries of the milk market. She and Daniel toured the state checking possibilities: vineyards, Indian corn, micro-breweries, and more. They stumbled on Orb Weaver (see chapter 5) and liked what they saw. They went on to check out the goat cheesemakers and talked to

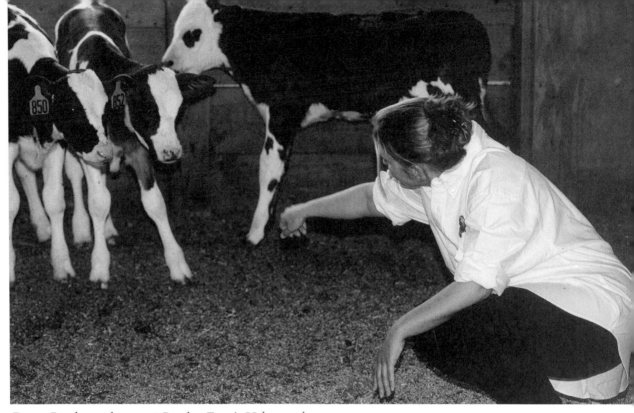

Dawn Boucher with some of Boucher Farm's Holstein calves

Allison Hooper of Vermont Butter and Cheese Company (see chapter 4).

Dawn had been making stovetop cheese in her kitchen for three years. Inspired by Allison's ideas, she began experimenting with a recipe for blue cheese. When a proposal was made at one of the farm's regular Saturday-morning business meetings that they increase the size of the herd, she and Daniel countered with a proposal to diversify instead. Her kitchen-made cheese was good enough by that time to impress her business-oriented in-laws. They agreed to finance a new cheese house next door to the cow barn. As Daniel said later: "It didn't cost as much as a new tractor."

While Daniel and his brother built a roomy, bright facility, designed with the help of Byron Moyer and his state inspectors, Dawn refined the recipe for Green Mountain Blue Cheese. Finding equipment was challenging, but Daniel managed to come up with a covered, square cheese vat that can hold 4,000 pounds of milk and is only 33 inches off the floor, ideal for the petite cheesemaker.

By the time the facility was fully equipped and inspected (Doug Marsden, the inspector, gave it the first 100 percent approval of his career), Dawn was ready to make cheese. She now makes it once a week, usually on a Tuesday. Daniel installed a flex pipe that takes off from the vacuum milking system before the milk reaches the bulk tank. The other end of this pipe goes directly into the cheese vat. At about 4:30 A.M., when Dawn yells over to Daniel in the barn that she is ready, he simply turns a valve and the raw milk flows directly from the cows into her cheese vat at a perfect 80 degrees without using artificial heat. When her vat is full enough (1,000 to 1,500 pounds is plenty now) she shouts for Daniel to turn it off, stirs in her culture, covers the vat, and lets it incubate for two to three hours.

This gives her time to go back to her spacious newly built house to grab some breakfast and maybe a nap. When she returns to the cheese room, she adds rennet and 1 drop of Roquefort blue from France. After she cuts the curd, she shovels it all into bucket molds lined with cheesecloth and lets them all sit in the whey for about an hour and a half. Then, using metal S-hooks, she hangs the cheesecloth bags around the edge of the vat and lets them drain until 7:30 that night. At about that time, she fills 1-gallon containers with water and places one on top of each cheesecloth bag to add further pressure for the rest of the night. (See also Ruth Anne Barker in chapter 4.)

Early the next morning Dawn weighs the pressed curd, mills it by hand, adds salt, and leaves it in the cheese room at 65 degrees for two more days. She takes it from there into the full basement they have built under the cheese room, where it goes into the brining room for two more days at 55 degrees. Then she finally packages it and takes it down the hall to the aging room, which is cooled to 42 degrees. They have three aging rooms, each capable of handling 5,000 pounds of cheese.

Dawn uses the same recipe for the Gorgonzola as she does for the blue, but she presses the curd around the sides of the mold as if it were a piecrust. The remaining milled curd she pours into the center and lets them stay that way for two months, turning each one every two days. She then removes them from their molds, and they age another four months, sitting on their shelves like so many cabbage-sized white peonies.

The blue is so pernicious that she can hardly keep food in her home refrigerator. It turns blue almost overnight. Despite rigorous cleaning it has coated the floor and crept partway up the walls of the cheese room. If it continues to do this, she won't have to inoculate anything: it will take care of itself. Mold also ranks high on the list of her private horror stories, but her worst experience was the petroleum-chemical taste some of her early cheeses suffered from.

"I went around licking everything," she recalls, "walls, floors, valves, pipes, and finally traced it to the plastic wrap I was using to hold the cheese while it aged."

Everyone on this highly organized farm has special responsibilities: Daniel does all the milking in a milking parlor that he has designed and installed for 16 cows at a time, each with her own "weigh jar" with which he monitors her production. His brother does all the fieldwork, and Dawn, in addition to making cheese, does all the tax work for the farm. She does not, however, consider herself a scientist.

"I definitely think that making cheese is an art form," she says. "If it were a super-technical science, I could never do it."

She does monitor the pH of the incoming milk because when it gets too high, she has to change her recipe. They have found that the pH of the milk reflects the acidity of the feed the cows are given. She tells Daniel when it goes up, and he changes the mix of cow feed that he's using. They grow and dry all their own corn for the grain and use round bales of hay, which they chop up and mix with the grain and the other ingredients for maximum milk production. Manipulating the quantities of each item changes the acidity.

Although University of Vermont professor Paul Kindstedt tells them that the growth hormone rBGH won't affect the cheese, they don't use it because of its cost and the hard sell that comes with it. Besides, everyone on their farm is environmentally conscious. If there's the slightest chance that what they are doing will harm the environment, they will look for another way to do it. "The finest food is found closest to its point of origin," says Dawn in her cheese brochure. They go to a great deal of trouble to protect that "point of origin."

They also take good care of their neighbors and friends. Outside the cheese room is an ordinary refrigerator, which contains a collection of Dawn's cheeses. There is a note on the door telling people to help themselves. They either leave a payment or pay later.

Both Daniel's and his brother's homes and the milking parlor are heated by outdoor wood-burning furnaces whose heat is blown into the buildings through long underground ducts.

One of the most striking things about the farm is its openness: large, well-maintained buildings, new homes with lots of open space between. Except in the woods lining the fields in the far background, there are no trees. For just an instant you might think you were in Iowa, not just a few miles from the Canadian border in northwestern Vermont.

Joanne James with some of her Toggenburg goats

Lakes End Cheese
Misty Cove Pure; Misty Cove Blended

Two years of hard work preceded by three years of exhaustive planning have finally allowed Joanne James of Alburg, Vermont, to introduce her first and only cheese to the steadily expanding roster of this state's artisanal cheeses. Assisted by her family, her two Jersey cows, and her five Toggenburg goats, she has made this dream a reality.

Located just 3 miles from the Canadian border on the string of tiny Lake Champlain islands that are knitted together like a necklace of small beads by the winding thread of U.S. Route 2 north, Lakes End Cheese is responsible for putting the James family back into the business of farming. When Joanne married into this family 20 years ago, the last of its several farms in this area had just given up farming after nearly a century of dairying.

Fifteen years ago Joanne created her first business here by starting Shoreline Chocolates, now a successful small business manufacturing and selling hand-crafted chocolates. Joanne is the sole employee of Shoreline Chocolates, making them, packaging them, and marketing them partly by mail order and partly out of a small, compact store she and her husband built a few yards off a narrow but heavily traveled tourist route into Canada.

Five years ago, when a friend gave her some goat's milk, she decided to make some cheese. When the process turned out to be much more difficult than she had expected, she felt challenged enough to find out how to do it right. That led to three years of study and research that culminated in a small but beautifully laid out, fully equipped barn not far from where the old family barn had once been located.

Then came the cheesemaking facility that her husband built for her as an extension to the one-woman chocolate factory and salesroom. Much of the necessary equipment—hot water cooker, bulk tank, sinks, can cooler, and so on—they found in storage from former farming days. Her husband, a furnace maintenance specialist, installed it with professional care under the watchful eyes of the state inspectors, who were, as usual, nothing but helpful. Both the bright, spacious milk room in the barn, with its 250-gallon bulk tank for the cow's milk and its can cooler for the goat's, and the tightly compact cheesemaking room are spotlessly clean.

"Boy, do I do a lot of cleanup!" says Joanne.

Because she wants to make her facility available to anyone interested in seeing a real working farm and functioning cheese plant in full operation, all buildings are easily accessible, and there are large windows through which visitors can see it all happening.

Except for some help she gets from her son, who milks the cows before going off to work with his father, Joanne does everything herself. Two or three times a week, she transfers the cow's and goat's milk she plans to use that day into plastic containers and hauls them the few yards from the barn to the cheese room in a small tractor-drawn cart. In winter, she uses a sled. At the cheese room she pours the milk into the cooker.

The process is much the same as it is for any cheesemaker, moving the rounds of cheese into the brine after they come from the mold and three days later loading the 22- to 23-pound wheels onto a drying rack, where they stay for five days before being sealed with a thin layer of clear plastic. They then join their predecessors in a carefully cooled and humidified aging room, where they sit side by side like huge puffy cushions for approximately five months before they are offered for sale. They have by then become a luxurious burnished red-brown in color.

When Joanne first began to make cheese, she decided to take the advice of Marjorie Susman and Marian Pollack at Orb Weaver and concentrate on just one kind. But after many months of agonized care and waiting, she was not happy with the results. She is still suffering from the memory of having to bury 100 or more 23-pound wheels of her first mistakes. Something was missing and she couldn't find it, so she called the invaluable Peter Dixon. As he has often done, Peter managed to, as Joanne says, "tweak it right up."

A friend of hers has designed a web page on the Internet where she plans to make her product available. Also, she has cut the big wheels into various-sized wedges, which she has vacuum packed at a facility not far from her farm. These she distributes to various small retail outlets and general stores within easy reach. She also ships her 23-pound daisy wheel all over the country by UPS.

The barn at Blythedale Farm

CHAPTER 6

The Cheesemakers of Northeastern Vermont

BLYTHEDALE FARM

Vermont Camembert; Vermont Brie; Green Mountain Gruyère; Cookeville Parmesan; Jersey Blue

Born in Columbus, Ohio, Karen Galayda loved growing up in Lakewood on the west side of Cleveland. Her grandfather owned a small grocery store not far from her home. She used to look forward to visiting him because she got to drive past the stockyards where she could see all the animals. Nobody told her why they were there, but she vividly recalls seeing the sides of beef hanging in her grandfather's meat locker. After more than 15 years of farming and cheesemaking, she now understands the connection between the two.

Her family moved to Detroit in 1966. "I'll never go back

there!" sums up her time in Detroit. An abiding interest in horses drew her east. She found work in the restaurant business and became a professional groom at the polo grounds. To improve her income, she took a part-time job at one of the few small, well-preserved farms on Boston's North Shore. The farm manager, a young native Vermonter named Tom Gilbert, had grown up on his family's dairy farm in Springfield and was hoping someday to be able to afford one of his own.

The Hollanders, owners of this beautiful little coastal farm, were desperate to do something besides lose money with their 20 Jersey cows. Making cheese sounded like a good idea, and they offered Karen and Tom a chance to develop a salable Camembert.

Tom went to school and after an experimental period, he and Karen were able to put Craigston Camembert on the market. This acquired an excellent reputation in Massachusetts and the rest of New England, but because it was the only farm left in an area of expanding urbanization it became increasingly impractical.

When it finally closed down in 1992, Karen and Tom decided to keep the cheese part alive. They moved everything to Blythedale Farm in Springfield, Vermont, where Tom had grown up. His parents were in the heifer replacement business so they bought all their heifers and went on making the Camembert, now called Vermont Camembert. In order to reach a larger buying public, they added Vermont Brie.

Unfortunately, after a year or two it became impossible to sustain the cheesemaking operation in Springfield. They needed a farm of their own and quickly. The only thing available that they could afford was a 50-acre piece in Corinth with a house and barn—all that was left of 120 acres that was being sold in pieces. They took it and, in an absolute nightmare that neither of them wants to remember or repeat, moved their animals and all the cheesemaking equipment to Corinth.

Every day, Tom used to carry 800 pounds of milk in cans up the hill between the barn and the new cheesemaking facility they had to build. Until he pulled his back out. Now he pumps the milk up from two bulk tanks in the barn. They make cheese five days a week, alternating the kind depending on demand.

Of all their cheeses, Karen loves the Jersey Blue best because it's what she calls "middle cheese." Not hard, not soft. "It isn't a Cheddar but it's made like a Cheddar."

The cheese room itself is quite large and off limits to everyone except the two of them. People who want to watch them at work can do so through the long window that separates the packing/office area from the cheese room. From there you can watch them stirring the curd in the six fairly small vats, ladling out the whey, and pouring it down the two tables that slant together at the center, allowing the liquid to sluice off to the floor where a drain catches it and pipes it into an underground tank. On the way there, it passes through a small outside gravel pit where the birds remove all the solids.

Tom Gilbert with some of Blythedale's Jerseys

Their normal workday begins in the barn at 4:30 A.M. Tom does the milking while Karen grains the cows and takes care of the young stock. Because the artificial inseminators don't want to bother with such a small herd, Tom breeds his heifers the old-fashioned way. He raises the bull calves to be sold as veal or as pasture bulls.

One drawback to their lifestyle, Karen finds, is the lack of time for horseback riding. She, who used to ride 8 or 10 times a day, is now reduced to an occasional canter on the one horse she has left.

By eight o'clock they're in the cheese room, where they work steadily until one in the afternoon. The rest of the day is for packing, bookkeeping, trips to town, and milking again at 4:30. In summer Tom cuts hay, which they contract out for baling in round bales. They are both convinced that round bales are perfect for the small stony fields of Vermont, but they have discovered that when the cows are fed the round bales, the milk is not good for some of the cheeses, especially the Mountain Gruyère.

"There is a seasonal difference in the milk," she admits. "Winter milk is sweeter but I think it is because of the cows themselves, not their feed." She also points out that in winter everything slows down. "Brie and Camembert have to drain longer. It takes longer to ripen everything."

When people ask Tom what it takes to make a superior cheese, his answer is always the same: "Worry. A whole lot of worry!"

Mary Ella Farm

After long months of uncertainty, Harvey and Mary Ella Carter have landed on their feet. They outgrew their farm in Heath, Massachusetts, and, after a long search, finally found one they liked in Vermont. So they sold the farm in Heath and entered into a purchase and sales agreement for the new one. A few days before closing, the deal fell through, leaving the Carters with 100 sheep and no farm. In a desperation move, they relocated temporarily on a small unused farm a few miles from Dorset, Vermont, where Mary Ella had grown up. Cheesemaking was impossible there, so Mary Ella cared for her animals and hoped for a miracle. It, the miracle, arrived in March 2000 when they found a 222-acre farm, 1,560 feet up on an open hill in Corinth Corners, Vermont.

These are not young people. Boyish, energetic, irrepressibly optimistic Harvey has been teaching part time for the past 15 years, which has left him free to do fieldwork and help with the animals in summer. Mary Ella is a sweet, compact, gentle woman with a will of iron. She has two grown daughters by a first marriage; Harvey has two grown sons. She also holds a graduate degree in soil science from Cornell University. At the Ithaca Farmer's Market they met Jane North of the Northland Sheep Dairy in Marathon, New York, and fell in love with sheep's milk cheese.

It was inevitable that they should meet Cindy and David Major of Vermont Shepherd, who advised them to go to the Basque region of southern France and talk to Luci Oxandabaras. They did, and when they returned to this country in 1995 they acquired a flock of mixed-breed dairy sheep from the Norths. Mary Ella, who does all the cheesemaking, made the cheese she learned in France, one similar to Vermont Shepherd, and sold it by mail order and word of mouth.

"I hate selling," she declares. "I'd much rather barter."

Their new cheesemaking operation is producing aged raw milk cheese. In just one summer they have accomplished wonders with this old farm. A milking facility overlooking the gently sloping pastures and a large, sunny, fully equipped cheese room have been completed. The latter includes a separate drying area and a huge aging room where consistent temperature and humidity are maintained year-round by an air exchanger that brings fresh air in from the outside and circulates it through all the rooms, eliminating gases en route.

Special racks hold the curing cheeses. They are made from kiln-dried ash because Mary Ella feels strongly that ash is the best wood for curing cheese. Upstairs in this brand-new building is a spacious room to hold Mary Ella's two large looms. She makes cheese in the summer and does her weaving in the winter. There is also room for a small retail store, which they will stock with their own products and sell to visitors.

As she reminisces about making cheese, Mary Ella says that despite her scientific background she's really not much for "whistles and buttons."

Mary Ella Carter knows each one of her sheep by name.

"I do it mostly by the smell and feel and taste," she explains. "Every day is different."

In the summer, what Mary Ella calls her "hefty girls" are watched over by the two Maremma dogs, Mario and Tomba, who not only look like sheep but think they are sheep. Eventually, they hope to milk between 50 and 60 ewes and make 1,700 to 2,000 pounds of cheese each year.

Their arrival in Corinth Corners has turned this small village into a major farmstead cheesemaking community. Only a few miles down Goose Green Road from their farm, Abe Jacobs Road turns off and a mile later puts you right into Cookeville, only a few hundred yards from Blythedale Farm's herd of Jersey cows. Visitors can choose between high-quality cow and sheep cheese, both made right there.

BONNIE VIEW FARM
Bonnie View Feta

In what is known as Vermont's Northeast Kingdom lives the most distant member of the Vermont Shepherd "family": a tall, raw-boned young native Vermonter with a degree in mechanical engineering whose name is Neil Urie. Brought up on his father's 100-cow dairy farm, he bought his present 470-acre spread from his uncle in 1993 after he returned from a session in the Peace Corps in Jamaica.

He stocked the old barn with 60 or 70 Holsteins and for five years fol-

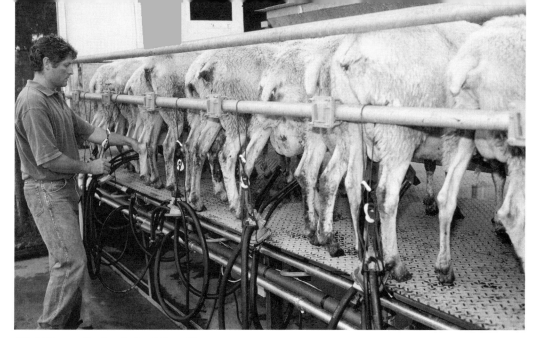

Neil Urie milks his flock of East Friesians.

lowed in the family footsteps. Then he began to think how nice it would be not to milk in winter and maybe even have some control over his final product and its price. What Cindy and David Major were doing seemed to provide an answer.

So he sold the cows and bought a flock of East Friesians from Major Farm. Building a bright, nearly open-air milking parlor took a little more than a year. The plastic sides roll up in hot weather to afford better ventilation.

The farm spreads out into large, flat, open fields on both sides of the road. You feel as if you were on a high plateau fringed by mostly deciduous woods.

There is no other house in sight, and practically no traffic passes. Neil built a small cheese house across the road from his old farmhouse. He's now milking 140 ewes from May through October and hopes to increase to 160. He figures that he might actually make a small profit, which he never did milking cows.

Neil never really learned how to make cheese. The first year he brought in an intern couple who had apprenticed with the Majors, and now his neighbor, Victoria Von Hessert, has become his more or less permanent cheesemaker. She pretty much learned her craft on her own. She read some books, worked briefly with Kathy Bixler, the English cheesemaker who appears in Vermont from time to time, made some mistakes, and has over time gained the skill and confidence to make a fine Vermont Shepherd and an excellent Feta. Neil has storage for about a week's worth of cheese. Then, helped by his sister in Townshend and sometimes his mother, he makes the long trip south to the cave. In deference to his Scottish heritage, he embosses a thistle on each wheel and looks forward to developing his own special cheese.

He is a tall man in a low-ceilinged house.

UP A CREEK CHEESE COMPANY
Belgian Abbey

Marybeth and Frankie Whitten have recently landed on their feet again after losing their sheep and their cheesemaking facility when the department of agriculture commandeered their flock in 2000 (also see Three Shepherds of the Mad

River Valley in chapter 4). Located not far from Bonnie View Farm, the Whittens now buy the milk they need from Neil Urie's large herd of sheep. They have just begun making their popular Belgian Abbey cheese again and should have it ready to sell by fall 2002.

Frankie, born in Greenville, South Carolina, went to Sterling College in Craftsbury, Vermont, where he met Marybeth. After completing their bachelor's degrees at the University of Maine, a job opened up at the Old Chatham Sheepherding Company in New York, the world's largest sheep dairy. Marybeth and Frankie snapped it up. While they didn't make cheese at Old Chatham, they did gain in-depth experience with sheep.

While working at Old Chatham, they discovered that the Freeman family of Stowe was looking for a way to reactivate their picturebook farm at Skunk Hollow in Greensboro. Although the farm had not been used for 20 years, the buildings and grounds had been kept in mint condition. The Whittens proposed that, given the chance, they could manage a cheesemaking facility there that would not only pay for the investment but would in time make a small profit. Anxious to keep the farm alive but wary of a cow dairy, the Freemans agreed to build a milking parlor and a separate cheesemaking building, and to finance the acquisition of 52 East Friesian ewes imported from Belgium.

Meanwhile Marybeth and Frankie, who had met Dave and Cindy Major of Vermont Shepherd while working at Old Chatham, apprenticed at the Majors' Sheep Dairy Center in Putney. They also took Paul Kinstedt's intensive cheesemaking course at the University of Vermont and helped supervise the design and construction of the new buildings. In a remarkably short time they were supplying a substantial amount of top-quality cheese to Vermont Shepherd.

Eventually, the long haul from Greensboro to Westminster West to deliver the wheels of Vermont Shepherd became oppressive. With the help of Larry Faillace of Warren and Freddy Michiels, a cheesemaker brought over from Belgium by the Freemans, Marybeth and Frankie began to develop their own cheeses. But their budding success was abruptly terminated by the government quarantine.

They are now completing construction on a new facility located in Albany, only an eighth of a mile from Rivendell Meadows Farm.

RIVENDELL MEADOWS FARM

Goat Chèvre; Goat Feta

Like any good hobbit hole, this farm is well protected. You will never sneak up on Keith Kirchner and Karlin Ostenfeldt. Two pugnacious geese will announce your arrival at high volume. It was not their intention to wind up on top of a high ridge in the Northeast Kingdom, whose growing season is too short for tomatoes and peppers and where the temperature in winter is frequently 35 degrees below zero.

Keith and Karlin shut down their farmstead goat cheese facility in Michigan because the state regulatory agencies were hostile to small operations. While investigating Vermont as a possible new home, they found not only a friendly reception at the state inspector's office but actual assistance. Unfortunately, the sale of the farm they thought they were buying fell through at the last moment. Like Mary Ella Carter, they had to settle for what they could find.

This turned out to be a 200-year-old abandoned 133-acre farm on a beautiful but unforgiving ridge in sight of the Canadian border. So they drove 8,000 miles over the course of several trips from Michigan to Vermont and spent more than $30,000 to get their goat cheese business reestablished in the Northeast Kingdom. By frantically loading up two 53-foot semis, a 50-foot double-decker livestock van, a pickup with a flatbed trailer, and a car also pulling a trailer, they managed to move everything they couldn't sell and begin a costly two-year period of restoration. The farm had no water, no electricity, and no floor in the sagging, falling-down house.

"I don't know how we got through that," Keith says, looking back. "I'd never do it again."

That was eight years ago. Eight years spent rebuilding the small, old, timber-framed house from the inside out, replacing all the plumbing, rewiring both the house and the 200-foot barn, and running 2,500 feet of water line from a spring they share with a neighbor. In the process they lost two years' income and had to start their cheese business all over.

They spent four years making goat cheeses. Karlin milked between 60 and 65 goats and did most of the work with the 120-plus animals in the herd. Keith was the cheesemaker, packager, marketer, distributor, and cleanup crew all in one. He also cut and baled 5,000 bales of hay a year and did all the fieldwork.

Rivendell supplied all the goat Feta for the many training restaurants operated by the New England Culinary Institute in addition to many others in southern New England and the Midwest. After that, they were exhausted. They had burned themselves out and as a result diverted what energy they had left into the manufacture of goat's milk soap, thousands of 4.8-ounce bars of soft, scented soap that need no refrigeration. They canceled all their cheese contracts, sold all but 25 or 30 of their animals, and now make just enough chèvre and Feta for a few of their best Vermont customers.

Keith has a degree in biology and spent 13 years managing a hazardous substance and toxic waste analysis lab in the Midwest. When the company was sold and subsequently downsized, he went into organic vegetable growing, supplying produce for Detroit, Toledo, and Cleveland. Then came the goats: Angoras for their fiber. When in 1990 the price dropped from $7 a pound to 63¢, he got out and went into goat's milk and goat's milk cheese and thence to Vermont.

He much prefers used equipment that he can fix up. When it comes to purchasing a piece of machinery, he always asks himself how many hours of labor it will save him and balances that with its cost. Needless to say, he does not own a computer.

Even with all of its power outages, he says, there are a couple of good things about the area: it has incredible fall foliage and is one of the best cross-country skiing spots in the country. Perhaps now that they have downsized their operation, he and Karlin will find the time to enjoy it.

The Lazy Lady Farm

Valençay; Les Pyramides; LaRoche; Capriola; Mon Jardin; LeBrique; Chèvre au Lait; Snyderbrook Jack; Capridos; Peppermid; Petit Tomme; Gran Tomme; Sagebrush; Nutzola

Far down the hill from Rivendell lies the Lazy Lady Farm. There used to be a handwritten sign on the front door of the unpainted, newly built house:

> BLESSED ARE THE CHEESEMAKERS
> ORGANIC ARTISANAL GOAT CHEESE
> DELICIOUS, ORGANIC, PASTURE-RAISED
> LAMB, HAND WOVEN APPAREL

Old Sabu, the Lazy Lady's Airedale kind of dog, watches over a small flock of goats and sheep in a new-looking, open-sided shed next to a compact barn. There are solar panels on the roof of the house. Some beehives next to a vegetable garden. It is quiet. Very quiet.

Laini Fondiller, the Lazy Lady, hand milks 16 registered French Alpine, Nubian, and Nupine goats and makes a dozen or so cheeses in the small compact cheese room, an add-on to one side of the house and just a few steps away from the barn.

Laini Fondiller convenes with her goats.

It was almost 14 years ago that she saved enough money to talk Barry, who owned this small acreage, into pooling their resources, building the house and barn, and digging the cheese cave. "We just dug a big old hole in the hillside in the woods below the house," she says. "Never even hit a rock."

With its arched ceiling, the cave looks like a miniature cathedral. The cement walls were hand poured, one bucket at a time. They keep the temperature at 58 degrees in summer and 45 degrees in winter. When it gets too dry in winter, Laini throws a bucket of water on the floor. There is an open duct above the thick front door that lets all the spores from the woods drift into the cave, often causing riotous color combinations on some of her aged cheeses.

Lazy Lady Farm began with a vegetable garden. Then they bought seven sheep, and Laini started to weave and make felt. When a goat joined the group, she began to make cheese in her kitchen and sell it at the local farmer's market. Then she added two more goats, and then six, and still she made cheese in her kitchen.

Laini and Barry eventually added a cheese room to the house in order to meet state health requirements. The state also insisted that she have a pasteurizer. Even if they could afford $15,000 for a pasteurizer, solar power was not sufficient to run one. The state persisted until Laini went out and gathered 250 signatures, hired a lawyer, and held her own public hearing.

The health department relented enough to allow Barry to build a small pasteurizer. If after a month of daily tests it lived up to the very specific regulations governing pasteurizers, they would allow Laini to make cheese with it. Using a couple of kitchen pots and a lot of ingenuity, Barry assembled a pasteurizer that had a cover and held a gallon or two. It passed all the tests without any trouble; Laini is using it to this day.

"I still would someday like to make raw milk, semiripened cheese," she muses, "and have a special label."

Things are a little easier for her these days because the folks at Provisions International (see chapter 1) have talked her into letting them distribute her products throughout the state. This is a good example of the closeness of the Vermont cheese community. Her neighbors and benefactors at Butterworks Farm, an organic dairy farm that makes and distributes yogurt, take her cheese with them on their weekly run downstate and drop them off at the Upper Valley Food Coop in White River Junction, next door to Provisions' warehouse.

Laini stops making cheese every January. "I find cheesemaking a burnout job!" She moves her felting table into the cheese room and, using the wool she sheared the previous spring, spends the winter weaving and making felt.

Some people live lives that have been carefully thought out and planned, but Laini got to where she is by means of an interrupted Great Circle Route. An orphan at age 21, she hated Indiana, where she was born. After attending college there she went east and got a job on a hog farm in Massachusetts. She learned tractoring, animal husbandry, and how to stone a field. A good friend was an agricultural extension agent and taught her dairying on his dairy farm. In 1979 she drove up to Vermont and started knocking on farmhouse doors looking for work. For two years she worked at various farmhand jobs.

When two friends offered to take her to France with them, she accepted. Unfortunately, she spoke no French. Her friends gave her a card on which they had written, in French, "I am an American. I don't speak French. Can I work here?" Armed with that card, she began knocking on farmhouse doors. One of them let her in and gave her work on a dairy farm. They also taught her to speak French. A member of that family, Girard, is now a neighbor of hers here in Vermont. When she wanted to learn how to make goat cheese, Girard found an advertisement for a goat dairy on the island of Corsica. He called them up and they agreed to take Laini.

This became her first cheesemaking job. She machine milked 250 goats and made raw milk cheese. They used no cultures but saved a little whey from each batch and used it as a starter for the next. She spent two years there, working with both goats and sheep, using ancient, hand-me-down recipes for cheese, not all of which worked very well. Then the law caught up with her because she had no papers. "Corsicans are nuts," she says today. Back in the States in 1984, she ran into Jack Lazor of Butterworks and went to work in his yogurt factory.

When people advise her to increase her herd, she replies: "I don't want to milk more goats, and I don't want to make more cheese than what I'm doing." When they remind her that the first law of business is that you must never run out of your product, she answers that that's fine if you're making Tootsie Rolls or aspirin; if specialty cheese runs out, however, it's a great opportunity for celebration when it comes back again.

She sells to only one restaurant because the owner comes up from Philadelphia to visit her for a few days every year and shovels manure and cleans stables and has a wonderful time. Mostly Laini does what Laini wants to do.

"I'm 47 now and hoping to keep it going till I'm 55," she says. "Then someone else can run the farm while I teach and take a day off."

The cheese cave at Vermont Shepherd

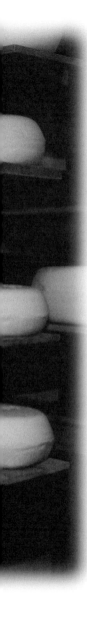

THE CHEESES

The "hefty girls" at Mary Ella Farm.

The Farmstead Sheep Cheeses

VERMONT SHEPHERD
Vermont Shepherd

When you cut into the light brown natural rind of Vermont Shepherd, the color of a 15-year-old maple tree, you're always surprised at the honey-smooth, nearly white interior. Aged four to six months, its complex, long-lasting flavor takes your palate through a range of experiences: back-of-the-throat richness; a mellow, haunting, slightly musty, full-bodied taste. There is nothing about it that suggests sheep. While it is not sharp, it is unique, definite, and memorable. This is a pear's best friend and is one of the few cheeses that can make a cheap wine taste like a rare vintage.

There is only one Vermont Shepherd. It was voted the best cheese in the United States at the annual cheese judging of the American Cheese Society in July 2000. The year before that, it was

Vermont Shepherd Cheese

Ingredients: Sheep's Milk, Lactic Cultures, Enzymes, Salt
Vermont Shepherd
875 Patch Road • Putney, VT 05346
www.vermontshepherd.com

voted best sheep cheese. It is elegant and distinguished, widely considered to be one of the finest cheeses in the world.

Three other cheeses are made and marketed under the same label. Two of them are made from cow's milk and are described in chapter 8. The other, also a sheep cheese, is called Shepherd's Tomme, and is available at a considerably lower price. While it differs little in flavor from Vermont Shepherd, it is not as pretty to look at. The rind may have blotches on it, or the interior may have spots of dark brown that need to be cut out. Often, however, it is just as good as its more expensive brother.

Peabody Hill
Woodcock Farm

This soft, rich, washed-rind cheese has a unique flavor without the slightest suggestion of sheep's milk. A washed-rind cheese means exactly what it sounds like. Gari and Mark Fischer spend a lot of time wiping the outside of each wheel with a wet cloth, to keep the rind soft throughout the aging process.

Peabody Hill comes in small plump wheels weighing approximately 2 pounds each. They will last in your refrigerator for more than six weeks, even after they're cut. But it will be gobbled up long before it turns blue or dries out. Its soft, melt-in-your-mouth interior is deep yellow like the color of heavy cream. While you can use it in cooking or on salads, this fine cheese stands on its own with a good Chardonnay and a few crackers. When you first catch sight of it, you might mistake it for Port-Salut or Saint-Paulin, but one taste will correct that impression. This has far more personality and distinction than either of those ancient French cheeses.

Weston Tomme
Woodcock Farm

This natural-rind sheep cheese has much the same consistency as Reblochon, the famous washed-rind cow cheese from the Haute-Savoie district of France. Drier and denser than Peabody Hill, largely because it is aged longer, its distinctive bite distinguishes it from other mellow, slightly musty-tasting cheeses.

Aged three to four months, it has none of the fruity flavor of Reblochon but tends to mature in the same way, growing harder, drier, and stronger with age. There is no taste of sheep in it though it lingers pleasantly on your taste buds, reminiscent of morel mushrooms. This is a red wine cheese and the near-perfect companion of a full-bodied California Zinfandel. Some of its flavor disappears when it is cooked; I don't recommend that you use it with macaroni.

It is available at the farmer's market in Londonderry and at one or two food coops in wedges or rough-surfaced wheels weighing 4 to 5 pounds. It's good for at least a month in your refrigerator if you wrap it in foil or waxed paper.

PIPER HILL
Woodcock Farm

Mark and Gari Fischer first created this excellent sheep cheese in the summer of 2000. A stronger, drier version of its sister, Weston Tomme, it has a distinctive back-of-the-mouth signature that has real staying power. Do not eat the rind, however. It won't hurt you, but it's not particularly tasty. They age this cheese longer than Weston Tomme, with the result that Piper Hill holds its unique piquant flavor when cooked. Try it in a quiche or an omelet. A rich Burgundy balances its flavor perfectly. You can purchase it in wedges or small, fairly thick 2- to 3-pound wheels that are usually smoother and lighter in color than the Tomme.

WEST RIVER SHEEP SUPREME
Woodcock Farm

This is Woodcock Farm's most recently developed cheese, and it is exquisite. Aged barely 60 days, it is a very soft natural-rind cheese with a cream-colored paste wrapped around a pure white center. Its faint evocative mustiness with just a touch of mushrooms, a hint of sour, and a haunting back-of-the-mouth feel that goes on and on is only equaled in my experience by Époise, the world-famous sheep cheese from the Rhone Valley of southern France. Indeed, you would be hard put to tell them apart.

Marinated Sheep Feta
Peaked Mountain Farm

Ann and Bob Works don't always make this lightly aged sheep Feta marinated in pure virgin olive oil with homegrown herbs and garlic. Like most marinades, you can use the oil for salads. They discovered the hard way that refrigeration causes the oil to become thick and cloudy and suggest that you keep it at room temperature. The herb-saturated oil will maintain the high quality of the cheese. Though not as sharp as some Fetas, it has significant bite even after a month or more in the oils. You will captivate discriminating guests by using it in pasta dishes. Or just serve it plain with Greek olives and crackers. When it is available, it is bottled in attractive 8- to 10-ounce glass containers.

Peaked Mountain Tomme
Peaked Mountain Farm

This is Ann and Bob Works's most significant accomplishment. Named after their farm in Townshend, Vermont, it is similar in appearance to Woodcock

Farm's Weston Tomme and Piper Hill, although the wheels are smaller and lighter in color. Peaked Mountain Tomme is a natural-rind, aged sheep cheese. It does not taste of sheep, and its distinctive voice reverberates pleasantly in your mouth. Haunting and evocative, it is a fine companion to a mature red table wine.

The flavor is too light to withstand cooking, but I took a wedge to France last spring and amazed some farmstead cheesemakers in the Rhone Valley. They could hardly believe that a pair of humble Vermont cheesemakers could make a cheese that was as good as or better than what they were making. Aged three months, it is available from midsummer through Thanksgiving at local food coops and farmer's markets.

Peaked Mountain Camembert
Peaked Mountain Farm

The most recent arrival in the pantheon of Vermont farmstead cheeses, this excruciatingly ripe sheep cheese is in that sublimely exclusive class that includes Willow Hill's Cobble Hill and Woodcock Farm's West River Sheep Supreme. However, just as these cheeses are delightfully different from each other, Peaked Mountain Camembert is different from both of them.

The first taste is a mouth-puckering tang; as that recedes, something faintly recognizable enters this blend of subtle flavors. Am I getting the taste of something blue? Yes, undeniably there is a thin but identifiable mist of Gorgonzola in the lingering aftertaste. I used to think that Old Chatham Sheepherding

Company's Sheep Camembert was the world's best. This world-class cheese makes me question that judgment.

Red Wax and Natural Rind Paisan Cheese
Three Owls Dairy

Of all the farmstead sheep's milk cheeses available in Vermont, these two Paisan (peasant) cheeses are in a class by themselves. The one dipped in red wax is young and soft and dry, with a gentle, pleasant flavor and an appropriate salty/sour ratio. This is a cheese that grows on you. And it really gains stature if taken out of the refrigerator at least an hour before being served. A solid and acceptable cheese for a wide range of tastes, this is also an excellent addition to any mildly flavored omelet or cream sauce.

Its companion cheese, sold unwaxed, has a beautifully gnarly natural rind that conceals a dark beige, quite dry and crumbly paste that is unexpectedly strong and deep in flavor. A little like Peaked Mountain Tomme and Woodcock Farm's Weston Tomme, it has more impact than either of them, although its power is perhaps not for everyone. Highly individualistic, natural rind Paisan more than holds its own on a cheese board in a mix of hard and soft goat and sheep cheeses, although I wouldn't serve it with a Cheddar. The two would fight each other, to the detriment of both. Unless you wish to frighten your guests, trim off the rind before presenting it. A pint of English porter or a dark ale makes a fine companion.

Autumn Oak
Willow Hill Farm

Willow Smart makes these small, flat, inch-thick, 1- to 2-pound rounds out of the organic raw milk from her mixed-breed flock of sheep. This cheese, which looks like a small Tomme, won an award at the 1999 American Cheese Society judging. The flavor is smooth, and the natural rind is light brown in color.

Instead of pressing the whey out, she ladles the curd by hand into molds and lets it drip overnight. She then ages it for 70 to 80 days in her own cave. She credits this time-consuming process with giving the cheese its smooth, almost silky texture. I don't recommend using it for cooking, however: Its flavor disappears almost completely when heated. It is best served at room temperature on a plain, crispy cracker. If you plan to have a wine with it, make it light, like a young Riesling. It is available from early summer through late fall in the Burlington Farmer's Market or at Willow Hill Farm in Milton.

Alder Brook
Willow Hill Farm

This is Willow's sheep's milk version of the well-known French cheeses Valençay and Pyramide, which are usually made from goat's milk. Like those two chèvres, she shapes Alder Brook into a small cut-off pyramid that weighs only 6 to 8 ounces. Very soft and mild, it is unique among sheep cheeses, which are seldom

Willow Smart's sheep cheeses aging in her cave

that young. It doesn't mix well with wine, making it the perfect cheese for teeto-
talers (even a thin, weak vintage leaches out the subtle overtones of this cheese's
delicate flavor). It looks great on a cheese board and works admirably with fresh
raw vegetables.

COBBLE HILL
Willow Hill Farm

This organic raw milk sheep cheese is my absolute favorite of all Willow's cheeses. Made only at the end of the milking season when the fat content of the milk is highest, it is so rich and creamy that is makes my mouth water just to talk about it. Aged in her cave for 60 to 70 days, it emerges still soft, just bulging at the edges. She doesn't make this every year.

Its piquant, slightly fruity flavor lingers and lingers after each bite, leaving a unique aftertaste somewhat similar to Woodcock Farm's West River Sheep Supreme described above, but more firm and dry. It is such a full and satisfying experience when eaten by itself on a sourdough baguette that I won't even suggest cooking with it. The fresh fruity taste of a good German Liebfraumilch makes an excellent accompaniment.

Cobble Hill is available in small puffed-up wheels weighing 1½ to 2 pounds, or in cut wedges that are swelled out against their wrapping. Willow's infinite care with these soft, delicious wheels pays huge dividends in terms of flavor and texture. Its brief season only sharpens your pleasure when it finally does arrive. You'll find it at the Burlington Farmer's Market and in several Vermont food coops or, if you wish, you can pick up some when it is available at her farm (see Appendixes).

The sheep's milk cheeses

1. *Weston Tomme (Woodcock Farm)*
2. *Mountain Tomme (Willow Hill Farm)*
3. *West River Sheep Supreme*
   (Woodcock Farm)
4. *Vermont Shepherd*
5. *Weston Tomme*
6. *Cobble Hill (Willow Hill Farm)*
7. *Vermont Shepherd*

The goat's milk cheeses

1. *Sage Brush (Lazy Lady)*
2. *Mon Jardin (Lazy Lady)*
3. *Goats-Milk Brie (KC's Kritters)*
4. *Fresh Herbed Goat Cheese (Vermont Butter & Cheese Company)*
5. *Vermont Bonne-Bouche Ash-Ripened Goat Cheese (Vermont Butter & Cheese Company)*
6. *La Roche (Lazy Lady)*
7. *Green Mountain Pepper Cheese (KC's Kritters)*
8. *Le Brique (Lazy Lady)*

The cow's milk cheeses

1. Crowley Cheese
2. Jesse's Middletown Cheese
   (Pomeroy Farm)
3. Green Mountain Gruyère
   (Blythedale Farm)
4. Vermont Farmhouse Cheese
   (Orb Weaver Farm)

5. Vermont Brie
   (Blythedale Farm)
6. Grafton Sage Cheddar
7. Grafton Cheddar
8. Sharp Cheddar
   (Shelburne Farms)

9. Maple Smoked Gouda
   (Taylor Farm)
10. Gore-Dawn-Zola
    (Green Mountain Blue Cheese)
11. Traditional Smoked
    Provolone (Westminster Dairy)

Members of the flock at Mary Ella Farm

*Sheep cheese curing in the cave
at Vermont Shepherd*

The Norman-style barn at Shelburne Farms

The kids are curious at Lazy Lady Farm

Goat cheese aging in the cave at Lazy Lady Farm

Aging wheels at Cobb Hill Cheese Company

Jersey cows give exceptionally rich milk

Peaked Mountain Farm

Summertomme
Willow Hill Farm

This summer version of Autumn Oak won first prize in the Mixed Milk category of the American Cheese Society competition in 2001.

As the name suggests, this unique creation is a celebration of July and August warmth and the herbs that flourish in those benign temperatures. It is Vermont's excellent version of the internationally famous Brin d'Amour made by the Basques on the island of Corsica. Soft, smooth, and pure white on the inside, it is rolled in dried herbs that flavor the interior over time. Willow's sheep get better feed than those of Corsica, however, since that Mediterranean island is covered mostly with brambles. This results in richer milk, which pays off with richer cheese.

I'm not saying that Summertomme is better than Brin d'Amour. While the two cheeses have some things in common, they are different in flavor. It is, however, fair to say that anyone who enjoys Brin d'Amour will enjoy Summertomme. It is especially delightful when accompanied by a fruity German May wine.

Mountain Tomme
Willow Hill Farm

I describe this mixed-milk cheese (30 percent sheep's milk, 70 percent cow's milk) in chapter 9, The Farmstead Cow Cheeses.

Belgian Abbey
Up a Creek Cheese Company

Marybeth and Frankie Whitten developed this classic Old World cheese while they were at Skunk Hollow Farm outside of Hardwick, Vermont, making sheep cheese for the Freeman Foundation. The nearly pure white insides are surrounded by a ¼-inch light brown rind. You might easily confuse its appearance with Vermont Shepherd, but one taste will set you straight.

It has a delicate, slightly nutty first flavor, which deepens into a mellow mustiness, a lingering earthiness that lasts a long time. At its peak—after about four or five months of aging—it feels moist and slightly soft.

This cheese is rare anywhere in the world but in Vermont is one of a kind, the perfect complement to a fine vintage Chardonnay. Belgian Abbey added to shirred eggs will elevate their flavor to memorable heights, although you will probably prefer to make it the centerpiece of an elegant cheese board.

Although Belgian Abbey was currently unavailable as this book went to press (see Up a Creek Cheese Company in chapter 6), look for the reappearance of this elegant sheep cheese by late summer or early autumn 2002.

Bonnie View Feta
Bonnie View Farm

Cheesemaker Victoria Von Hessert has come up with a fine sheep Feta. Her struggle was long and difficult, but the result is well worth waiting for. This is a firm, quite dry Feta. Not too salty, it is the mildest Feta made from sheep's milk that I have ever tasted. It is reminiscent of goat's milk Fetas made by KC's Kritters and Rivendell Meadows. Subtle and interesting, it won't steal the show when used in cooking.

CHAPTER 8

The Farmstead Cow Cheeses

FERNWOOD
Willow Hill Farm

Fernwood is Willow Hill Farm's world-class entry into the realm of soft cow's milk cheeses. Willow Smart brings organic Jersey milk down from Ann and Jack Lazar's Butterworks Farm in Vermont's Northeast Kingdom and turns it into a soft, magical cheese. It bears some resemblance to Fromage de Chlarines from France, or a mature Taleggio from Italy.

Delicious is too weak a word to express the power of its first flavor, and *mellow* understates the long-lasting back-of-the-mouth aftertaste: a delicate whiff of tannin and sweet bark. Willow created this remarkable cheese in the summer of 2000, and it is usually available year-round. For an exquisite moment of glory, try pairing Fernwood with a full-bodied merlot.

This cheese is a fine addition to any cream sauce or melted into a pasta with a little garlic and oil. In order to keep it soft and pliable, Willow ages it only the minimum 60 days. In a refrigerator, it retains its taste and texture best if wrapped with waxed paper or foil. Look for it at the Burlington Farmer's Market and the usual Vermont food coops.

Mountain Tomme
Willow Hill Farm

This aged mixed-milk cow/sheep cheese is quite different from all the other tommes in both form and taste. Unlike most tommes, this one has a spray of fine holes in its body. When you first put it in your mouth, nothing happens. The texture is pleasant and smooth, but there is virtually no taste. Then, quite suddenly, the flavor emerges: caramel with a quiet nuttiness, perfectly balanced with a subtle saltiness, like a well-made candied popcorn. The taste lasts a long time and begs to be matched with a Rhone Valley merlot.

Vermont Brabander
Three Shepherds of the Mad River Valley

Cheesemaker Jackie Faillace in Warren, Vermont, is still making this classic Belgian cheese from the organic milk of the nearby Von Trapp farm. The

Jackie Faillace inspects a batch of her cheese

chunky 4- to 5-pound wheels are somewhat rough on the outside with a rind the color of burnt ocher. Inside is a rich yellow paste that is semisoft and smooth. Because of the Jersey milk, which is higher in butterfat than any of the other common breeds of dairy cows, the cheese tastes just as rich as it looks. While it comes across as pretty mild in flavor, there is the echo of a wet autumn woods in the lingering aftertaste.

This thoroughly delightful cheese is quite at home with a lightly chilled Bordeaux Blanc. If you can get a '96 vintage, you will have one foot in heaven. Jackie's mother, Linda, stocks Brabander at the small, quaint country store she and her other daughter, Heather, operate just in front of the cheese facility where Jackie makes it. You have to bring your own Bordeaux, however.

Aurora
Three Shepherds of the Mad River Valley

This is Jackie Faillace's other cow's milk cheese. When young, it is somewhat similar to Colby. It has a washed rind and a texture that resembles Orb Weaver cheese (see page 160). When aged eight or nine months, however, it becomes a whole different cheese: Dry, nutty, deeply flavored, almost like a Parmesan, it simply takes over any other competition. Also, it will, as they say, melt in your mouth. The smooth flavor has more bite to it than the usual Colby. A pleasant table cheese, it comes in 2-, 6-, and 9-pound wheels. Served with Calamata olives, coarse French bread, and a good red wine, it will provide an excellent light lunch on a summer day. Linda tries to keep a fair amount on hand, but the demand often outruns the supply.

Jackie named this cheese Aurora because it reminds her of a summer dawn, and indeed there is that note of freshness about it.

Vermont Camembert
Blythedale Farm

This small 8-ounce, foil-wrapped cheese with a red ribbon around it was the first cheese made by Karen Galayda and Tom Gilbert when they became cheese-makers in Massachusetts. Now, two decades later, it is still just as smooth and rich as it ever was. Although Karen admits that a true Camembert cannot be made outside of France, hers needs no apology. Over the years it has built a faithful following and is the best-known Camembert being made in the United States today. Her small herd of pampered Jersey cows deserves full credit for the richness.

Northeast Cooperative distributes this fine cheese throughout New England and as far west as the Ohio River Valley. Serve it at room temperature with a crisp green salad and plain crackers. When you buy it, be sure you check the sell-by date on the back. Karen has an uncanny knack for naming the date on which the cheese will be at the peak of its flavor and texture.

VERMONT BRIE
Blythedale Farm

This is the companion cheese to the Camembert above, and marketed with the same look: a small 8-ounce foil-wrapped wheel distinguished from its neighbor by its kelly green ribbon. Slightly milder than the Camembert, it becomes truly delicious when wrapped in several layers of phyllo dough and baked for 15 or 20 minutes. Since there are no machines of mass production at Blythedale, these two fresh cheeses are extremely labor-intensive. A word to the wise: The Brie sell-by date is just as accurate as the Camembert. I've never lost one before the date, but you're on borrowed time after it.

Green Mountain Gruyère
Blythedale Farm

If your family likes macaroni and cheese, use this rich, nutty cheese when you make your next batch. Not as strong as Swiss Gruyère and without that trace of the bitterness that is part of the classic imported cheese, Green Mountain Gruyère can also be used to make a richly flavored fondue. Its melting characteristics are nearly perfect.

It is also remarkable for its shelf life. I have kept it in my refrigerator for more than a month with no mold problems and no perceptible loss of flavor. It improves with age, gaining in strength while still retaining its original nuttiness. It is not only a good cooking cheese but also is a welcome addition to any cheese board. Try it with a glass of Bourgogne Rouge '95 or '96. The two were made for each other. Aged four to six months, it is available in 5- to 7-pound wheels 2 or 3 inches thick with a light brown, somewhat coarse rind and a paste of smooth tan. In contrast to Swiss Gruyère, there are no small holes in it.

Cookeville Parmesan
Blythedale Farm

This is Vermont's only Parmesan, and one of very few being made in the whole country. Named after the township in which it is made, Cookeville Parmesan is a hard grating cheese. Like the other Blythedale cheeses, it is richer than other Parmesans, domestic or imported. Though not as strong as Italian Reggiano, it rivals Grana Padano and gets stronger as it ages. It is a full six months old before Karen Galayda and Tom Gilbert release it for sale. Even after that, it keeps on changing and a whole range of flavors develops after it is cut into wedges. A month after one of the 2-pound wheels is opened, it will be stronger, nuttier, and more biting.

Over the centuries, Parmesan and pasta have formed an unbreakable friendship. It's unusual to speak of one without the other. While almost any kind of red wine is acceptable with Parmesan dishes, it comes as no surprise that this primarily Italian package is best completed with a good heavy Chianti. Because of its strong, identifiable flavor you will find it in a great many hot dishes from clams to eggplant, but it seldom graces a cheese board.

Cookeville, like all Parmesans, is best when freshly grated. Be careful to wrap it tightly if you store it in your refrigerator. Because it has a low moisture content to begin with, double wrapping is a wise precaution against unacceptable dryness.

Jersey Blue
Blythedale Farm

According to Karen Galayda, this is the fussiest of the five cheeses she and Tom Gilbert make. Blue cheese is notorious for getting out of hand and contaminating the walls, ceilings, and floors of the cheese facility. Cleaning up takes almost as much time as making the cheese.

Jersey Blue took a first prize in the 1999 American Cheese Society competition. Unlike most blue cheeses, it is quite dry and crumbles easily. Only Colston Bassett Stilton from Neal's Yard Dairy in London is as dry as Jersey Blue. It is therefore an immense surprise when it suddenly melts in your mouth. Excellent on salads, it also cooks well. "If you want an outrageous sauce," says Rich Chalmers of Vermont Butter and Cheese, "mix Jersey Blue with crème fraîche." You will find none of the salty sharpness that is the trademark of most well-known blues, but it responds well to a glass of Portuguese Mateus. Its plump wheels are 5 to 6 inches in diameter and have light brown edible rinds.

Vermont Farmhouse Sharp Cheddar and Extra Aged Cheddar
Shelburne Farms

Cheesemaker Jamie Miller presides over a state-of-the-art cheese facility just a couple of hundred yards down the road from the restored, turn-of-the-20th-century barn that houses the purebred Brown Swiss cows that furnish the milk. His sharp Cheddar matches both Grafton and Cabot in quality, and every year the three of them pass around the first-prize trophy for the best Cheddar in the country.

In addition to vacuum-packed 40-pound blocks, he makes 23-pound daisy wheels that he wraps in cloth for further aging. After a year or more, he puts them out as an extra-aged Cheddar that matches or surpasses the best Cheddars from England. Originally developed by his predecessor, Ross Gagnon, it also has the distinction of tasting even better when it turns blue. Like Mrs. Appleby's Cheshire from England, it becomes a rare treat with a dry, slightly musty, altogether unique sharpness that stays and stays.

Accompanied by an ale from your favorite microbrewery or, if you're lucky, a '97 or '99 Beaujolais from St-Amour, Shelburne Farms Extra Aged Cheddar will make your cheese board literally fit for a king. Unfortunately, there's not a lot of this cheese available, but put your order in anyway. It's well worth waiting for.

The regular sharp Cheddar is available at Shelburne Farms, as well as at most of Vermont's food coops and gourmet cheese shops in handsome 1- and 2-pound waxed bricks.

Vermont Farmhouse Cheese
Orb Weaver Farm

This is one of the oldest farmstead cheeses in Vermont. Twenty years ago when Marjorie Susman and Marian Pollack first began production of this gentle, soft, Port-Salut-type cheese, there were only a couple of small cheese producers in the state. It is a good, reliable, soft, rich table cheese, the sort you have around for everyday use.

No wine is necessary to enjoy this Jersey Colby-style milk cheese. A slice of homemade bread, a chunk of Orb Weaver with a dill pickle added for color, and you have a simple, pleasant lunch. Add a light beer or ale on a hot summer day when you've just come in from the garden. It melts as if it had been born to melt: on hamburgers, with macaroni, on tomatoes, with scrambled eggs or a Denver sandwich.

Cave-Aged Farmhouse Cheese
Orb Weaver Farm

In the summer of 2000 Marjorie and Marian put aside a number of cloth-wrapped wheels of the cheese described above and let them age in their cave for a year or longer, in much the same way Shelburne Farms does with its Cheddar. After 12 to 14 months and several phone calls to *affineuse* Beth Carlson in Chicago, they removed the wheels from the cave. Their color was now dark brown. They were drier and imbued with an elegant sharpness that had not been there before. The poor peasant had become a wealthy aristocrat with a long-lasting, deep flavor that is not easily forgotten. This cheese won second place in its category in the 2001 American Cheese Society competition.

If you're lucky, you'll catch the two cheesemakers at the farmer's market in Middlebury, Vermont. They might have one or two of these amazing wheels with them. Or you can reserve one by calling them at the farm. Both the Vermont Farmhouse and the Cave-Aged make their way into a few of the Vermont food coops, the regular in either a 6-pound yellow waxed wheel or a 2-pound mini wheel.

VERMONT FARMSTEAD GOUDA
Taylor Farm

I love this cheese. It is so rich and special! Katie Wright has the touch of an old master even though she has been making it for only two years. This Gouda does everything right. Its strong initial impact slides lusciously into a great back-of-the-mouth taste that lasts and lasts. Not only does it melt beautifully, but it also holds its flavor when cooked.

It doesn't really matter what wine you pair it with because the cheese will steal the show; any pleasant-tasting red will be fine. Its texture is fairly soft, and the paste is sprinkled with small holes. Rich yellow in color from the milk of the Jersey cows Katie's husband, Jon, takes care of, it will last a long time in your refrigerator if you wrap it well.

Taylor Farm Gouda is available in fat 8- to 10-pound red waxed wheels at the farm in Londonderry, Vermont, and in several local farmer's markets and local food coops. This is a real family cheese guaranteed to disappear very quickly.

Maple Smoked Gouda
Taylor Farm

Katie and Jon Wright have their brown waxed Maple Smoked Gouda smoked at the Grafton Village Cheese Company. This won a third place in the 2001 American Cheese Society competition in Kentucky. There is something magical about the effect that smoking over a smoldering maple fire has on this cheese. It retains all of its fine original qualities while the maple smoke adds a unique dimension to its flavor. Even smoked Gouda from Holland or Bruder Basil from Germany does not compare with the excellence of this local product. The wheels are slightly flatter and about the same weight as the red waxed cheese. This is the perfect cheese for your family reunion. I guarantee there will be no leftovers.

PUTNEY TOMME
Vermont Shepherd

Nothing in its appearance will prepare you for the taste of this medium-hard cheese. The gray-brown, somewhat pitted natural rind of this dumpy 5-pound wheel looks less than promising. Even when you open it, the deep yellow-brown paste looks dried out and flaky.

Persistence pays, however. If you give up on it before trying it, you will have missed one of the finest taste experiences available in the world of cheese. The unpromising appearance conceals a cheese that literally melts in your mouth, leaving behind a complex of perfectly balanced flavors: slightly musty, pleasantly milky, and ideally salty. Married to a dry white Chilean wine, it will live in your memory happily ever after.

The only real weakness of Putney Tomme is its sluggish behavior in the oven. It doesn't cook well, but sprinkled on top of a quiche or a thick hearty soup it adds a delicious spurt of flavor. This is a natural-rind cheese aged four to six months in the Vermont Shepherd cave in Putney. The rind turns somewhat bitter during this curing process and should be removed before serving. It is available at Major Farm as well as at a few natural food outlets in southern Vermont. You will also find it at the Brattleboro Food Coop.

TIMSON
Vermont Shepherd

Cutting into this cheese is a wonderful experience. Beneath a soft beige rind you find a pure white paste. Your first thought is that you've made a mistake and cut into a goat cheese. One mouthful of this piquant softness with its late-blooming edge will bring you back to the land of cheese made with Jersey milk. Timson was out of production for several months, but has returned and is better than ever.

Because it is a washed rind cheese, the wheels of Timson are smaller than those of its companion, Putney Tomme. It melts well and retains its flavor in a cream sauce or an omelet. And it is strong enough to hold its own with a full-bodied Chardonnay or hearty Burgundy.

FOUR CORNERS CAERPHILLY
Cobb Hill Cheese Company

This Caerphilly-style cheese is the only one of its kind in Vermont. As I stared at the soft, plain surface of the newly cut wheel, with its light sprinkling of holes, it occurred to me that this cheese will probably gain a good deal of character if it were left to age for a few more months. The first taste confirmed this intuition. By the time this book is published, it should be just right. At the moment, it is quite mild and bears only a slight resemblance to the famous Welsh Caerphilly. Age often produces miracles, however, and this may be one in the making. I'll put a wheel away and we'll find out.

Ascutney Mountain Cheese
Cobb Hill Cheese Company

With this Appenzeller-style wheel made from Cobb Hill's Jersey milk, cheesemaker Marsha Carmichael has proved her skills. This is a stunning, unique cheese, different from but every bit as fine as the internationally known Swiss Appenzeller. It is a rich, deep yellow color, with a scattering of small holes. The nutty, sweet/sour taste spreads through your mouth, a feast for the taste buds. Then a wash of mellow, recognizable Swiss flavor emerges in the back of the mouth and lasts and lasts.

A fondue made with Ascutney Mountain will exhaust all superlatives. This elegant cheese is well worth a carefully chosen bottle of wine, perhaps a Beaujolais or a Liebfraumilch. Add some to the fondue, and drink the rest. I predict this cheese will be a strong contender of Best of Show at the American Cheese Society's annual judging this year.

Aged Raclette
Karen Bixler

This is a farmstead cheese at its most primitive. Made from the raw milk of one Jersey cow, mostly on the wood-burning kitchen range of an old farmhouse, it is aged in the basement. And it's good. It is in fact exceptional. Stronger than Swiss Raclette, drier and more pungent than French Raclette, it has a distinctive and lasting flavor. Raclette is generally thought of as the perfect companion for baked potatoes in what many Swiss call their national meal. In the Middle Ages the mountain farmers of Switzerland used to warm their cut wheels of Raclette in front of the open fire. When the surface began to run, they scraped the melting cheese onto their opened-up baked potatoes. Washed down with a mug of strong schnapps, it made the cold of winter a little less brutal. Now, of course, a fancy machine has been invented to melt the cheese and scrape it onto your potato. Certain exclusive restaurants will roll the machine to your table and perform the operation before your very eyes.

The lumpy little wheels of this Vermont Raclette look a little like aged Goudas when they are opened, quite dry and hard but still meltable. There is a hint of Gruyère in the aftertaste, along with an inevitable feeling of the cozy barn where the cheesemaker does her milking. Unless she happens to take it to a local farmer's market, you'll have to get it directly from her farm (see page 211).

Vermont Blue Cheese
Green Mountain Blue Cheese

Watching this cheese evolve has been an education in minor miracles. Cheesemaker Dawn Boucher originally described it as: "Twice the complexity of an earlier version . . . very spicy but not hot." Since then it has moved through a kaleidoscope of textures before ending up as the silky soft, smooth, fully marbleized blue-veined interior that it is now. If you crossed Great Hill Blue from Massachusetts with Cambozola from Germany you might come close to this creamy rich Vermont Blue cheese. Made from raw milk and aged four months, it has some of the bite of Danish Blue, but much more moisture and smoothness.

It also contrasts sharply with Jersey Blue, the other farmstead blue cheese being made in Vermont by Blythedale Farm (see page 158). Where Jersey Blue is rich and dry and crumbly, Vermont Blue is rich and soft and moist. The former is the color of thick farm cream, while the latter is the pure white of Italian marble. If you lined Vermont Blue up with Beenleigh Blue and Cashel Blue from England, Quezo Azur from the high Spanish Pyrenees, and Berkshire and Great Hill Blue, and tasted them all blindfolded, you would be able to identify Vermont Blue immediately.

This rewarding cheese is also extremely versatile: Spread it on a baguette or a crispy cracker, use it in a salad, add it to a creamy sauce for brussels sprouts or asparagus, and your meal is made. As for wine, Portuguese Mateus Rosé is a perfect match for Vermont Blue. If it's not available, a white Zinfandel from California also makes a good companion.

This extraordinary cheese is available in two or three Vermont food coops.

It comes in two cylinders, one weighing 1½ pounds and wrapped in a rich red foil; the other, in an intense blue or gold foil, weighs in at slightly more than 3 pounds.

Equally impressive is the new Gore-Dawn-Zola, a rich Gorgonzola that matches the quality of the imported Italian cheese of the same name. Look for the electric blue foil wrapper with the silver label.

NEIGHBORLY FARMS ORGANIC HOMESTEAD CHEDDARS
Neighborly Farm

Perhaps the most ambitious of Vermont's new farmstead cheesemakers is Neighborly Farms, which produces an impressive array of eight flavored

Cheddars and a cow's milk Feta. What's more, their cheeses are all 100 percent organic, but in contrast to most organic cheeses, their prices are quite reasonable. Their Cheddars come in a variety of flavors including garlic, hot pepper, salsa, chili, sage, and green onion. These mostly mild, semisoft cheeses are particularly appealing to children. In fact, a visit to Neighborly Farms is a perfect family outing. There visitors can walk down a windowed hallway between the barn and the cheese room and watch 30 Holsteins being milked on one side, while Linda makes cheese on the other. All of the cheeses are available for sale in a charming little store attached to the barn.

Jesse's Middletown Cheese
Pomeroy Farm

This tangy, slightly crumbly, green waxed cheese is another recent arrival to the steadily growing array of farmstead cheeses. It is aged a full nine months on Jesse Pomeroy's farm in the hills near Londonderry, Vermont, where his wife, Marian, makes the cheese while he runs the farm. Macaroni made with this cheese will get a standing ovation. It loses none of its tartness by cooking. Paired with a dry Italian Chianti, it will make an ordinary meal into a major event.

Although the Pomeroys, like the cheesemakers at Orb Weaver, have steadfastly refused to classify their raw milk cheeses in a traditional category, they can properly be described as table cheeses. Most cheeses, like most lovemaking, lose their glamour with overindulgence. Only a few can be consumed with consistent pleasure day after day. Even a Vacherin Mont d'Or or a Tumas d'la Paja will pale if served too regularly. Middletown Cheese, however, because it asks nothing of you, because it is not pretentious, because it is immensely flexible, can be served over and over in many different ways with many different wines or beer.

You'll find it at a couple of Vermont's food coops, and Marian takes it to the farmer's market—and, of course, it is available at their farm outside Londonderry (see page 54).

Misty Cove Pure and Misty Cove Blended
Lakes End Cheeses

From the northernmost tip of Lake Champlain, only 3 miles from Canada, Lakes End Cheeses offers two varieties of farmstead cheese. Misty Cove Pure is made solely from the milk of a small herd of Jersey cows. Four months of aging produces a mild, rich cheese with a pungent flavor that falls somewhere between an aged Gouda and a good Raclette. The taste of most mild and medium cheeses disappears soon after you bite down on them. Misty Cove Pure has great staying power. Even two or three minutes after you have eaten it, the flavor will still be there.

Joanne James, the owner, cheesemaker, and sole employee of Lakes End Cheeses, makes her second product from a 50:50 combination of Jersey milk from her cows and goat's milk from her herd of Toggenburg goats. She has named this cheese Misty Cove Blended and ages it somewhat less than the pure. The mixture produces a coarser version of the cheese with a salt/sour edge. It too has staying power.

These pleasant cheeses will go a long way toward brightening a cloudy day. Both of them melt well, making them fine for cooking, and both respond well to a good Merlot. Joanne has both available at her store in 23-pound daisy wheels or in approximately ½-pound vacuum packs. She has also placed them in some of Vermont's food coops and in several local markets in her area.

Fresh Mozzarella
Westminster Dairy

This is the first cheese developed at Peter Dixon's own cheese facility, Westminster Dairy. It is the only organic fresh Mozz available in New England. Sometimes called pulled Mozzarella because of the way it is made, it is somewhat coarser in texture and fuller in flavor than its commercial counterpart. True, it is not the pure white of the factory-made cheese because of the richness of the Livewater Farm Jersey milk from which it is made, but it more than makes up for this with its richness and genuine buttery flavor. Served with fresh basil and sun-dried tomatoes and drizzled with extra-virgin olive oil, it will more than delight any discriminating diner. It is also available smoked.

Traditional Aged Provolone and Smoked Provolone
Westminster Dairy

Peter Dixon's second cheese is the only organic Provolone in New England. It is almost as hard and dense a cheese as the Italian original and has a somewhat salty flavor. Again, the Jersey milk makes a much richer cheese than the usual Provolone, and because it continues to age the flavor becomes deeper and fuller to match the deep yellow color of the center. In keeping with Italian tradition, he shapes it into 1-pound pieces in the form of large pears that are hung from strings while they age.

Peter rubs the outside of the cheese with olive oil during the two months that he ages it, which not only burnishes the rind to an almost mahogany finish, but also flavors the cheese in a subtle and pleasing manner. He sends some of it over to Grafton, where they smoke it for him. The result is superb and is now the only organic smoked cheese available.

Asiago Fresco
Westminster Dairy

As far as I know, Asiago Fresco is the first organic Asiago made in the United States. Even when young and soft, it will more than pull its own weight with any pasta dish or quiche. With eggplant or veal parmesan it is outrageously fine. The first taste opens on a well balanced salt/sour ration, but after several moments the familiar asiago flavor begins to blook in the back of your mouth, where it continues to hold for some time. It is much more mellow than the typical raw, dry domestic Asiago, and presents a more striking personality than the traditional Italian Asiago.

In addition, this is a real habit-forming cheese. From its deep yellow color and its light sprinkling of holes to its rich softness, it is instantly addictive. A rich, dry Chianti would be the appropriate companion.

A member of Laini Fondiller's herd at Lazy Lady

CHAPTER 9

The Farmstead Goat Cheeses

FRESH CHÈVRES

The word *chèvre* is French and means simply: "goat." Nearly every goat cheesemaker who possesses a pasteurizer produces a fresh chèvre because it is easy and requires practically no aging. Several Vermont cheesemakers make fresh farmstead chèvres that require special mention.

Barker Farm

Ruth Anne Barker makes a tangy chèvre on her farm in Wallingford. Its flavor is pleasantly distinctive and has no hint of goatiness. There is a real distinction to be made here, however. Whereas most chèvre is crumbly, somewhat like a drier cottage cheese, Ruth Anne's has the texture of maple butter, and like most chèvres is fine for cooking.

KC's Kritters

Kevin Kingsley's chèvres are quite mild and crumbly. He is the only Vermont farmstead cheesemaker who adds flavors to his chèvre in the form of horseradish, herbs, garlic, or black pepper. Also, he is the only one producing a line of low-fat chèvres in the same flavors. All can be used in cooking, and all are pleasant additions to salads. But they are probably best enjoyed on a cracker or baguette.

Does' Leap Farm

This rich, creamy chèvre is deeply flavored and wholly memorable, comparing favorably to such internationally recognized chèvres as those from Coach Farms or Hawthorne Valley in New York State, Vermont Butter and Cheese Company in Vermont, and Bourdin, Couturier, and Montrachet in France. This fresh chèvre would enhance anything you served it with, whether bread and crackers, fresh vegetables, salads, or pasta. However, you will hardly surpass a bowl of this creamy chèvre accompanied by a glass of sherry, a guaranteed one-way ticket to heaven. Does' Leap packs their chèvre in olive oil with garlic and lemon thyme, where it will keep for several months without refrigeration. The oil makes a fine salad dressing even after the cheese is gone.

Rivendell Meadows

Rivendell Meadows makes a smooth, rich chèvre that is used in all the above ways and many more in several Vermont restaurants. If the chef in your favorite café is using it, he has a discerning taste and an eye for delicate flavor.

AGED CHÈVRES
The Lazy Lady

Laini Fondiller, the Lazy Lady (see chapter 6), makes 8 or 10 fine goat cheeses on her tiny farm in Vermont's Northeast Kingdom, barely a stone's throw from Rivendell Farms. She calls all of them chèvre, and subtle differences distinguish them. Valençay and Les Pyramides are both small truncated pyramids, one of which, the Valençay, is lined with ashes. If you close your eyes and play the tasting game with both, you will find them delicious, smooth, and mildly piquant. Despite the first prize awarded to the Valençay at the 1999 American Cheese Society judging, I doubt that you will be able to tell one from the other.

Then there are La Roche and Capriola, the former a cut-off cone shape, the latter larger than a button but smaller and thinner than a cupcake. Both are fresh, delightful, soft, and spreadable with slightly rough, beige exteriors. None of these small 4- to 6-ounce cheeses tastes remotely goaty, and all are ideal for a cheese board. If you fantasize strongly enough you can probably convince your friends that there is a difference in taste among them. Compared to other fresh goat cheeses there is a difference, but it is mainly one of degree.

In the subtle world of fresh or lightly aged goat cheeses, Humboldt Fog from Cypress Grove in California and Bucheron from France are considered the best. Those from Lazy Lady, however, are in a class by themselves. Her most recent triumphs include Mon Jardin, a beautiful Brin d'Amour–type cheese made with goat's milk, and Le Brique. The latter is a true rival to Humboldt Fog, complete with the line of ash in the middle. There is only one cheese in the country that surpasses it (see Flavored Goat Cheeses: Caprella, below). She also has one that is coated in sage that she of course calls Sagebrush. Then there are the cheeses she has aged for some time in her cave. Her most recent triumph is a holiday cheese called Nutzola that boasts a broad band of ground nuts running through the middle.

Chevraulait (pun intended) is a ¼-inch-thick, 3-inch-diameter patty with a forbidding rough exterior that darkens rapidly as it ages. Semisoft at first, it becomes harder and drier. This used to be a strong, goaty cheese that got goatier with time, though lately it has retained its strength but lost much of its goatiness. The same is true of Snyderbrook Jack, another patty-shaped cheese named after a small stream that runs through the Lazy Lady Farm. The only Jack cheese made from goat's milk, it is strong and sharp and goaty.

Capridos, however, is a different story. Made with raw milk, aged several months, this 8-inch wheel about ½ inch thick often acquires a rind that looks like a painting by Jackson Pollock. The outside is also very soft, almost mushy, but the smooth, creamy inside has only the faintest taste of goat. The rind acquires its coat of many colors quite naturally from the cave in which it is aged. Situated in the woods, it picks up fungi from the surrounding vegetation, which the cheese-maker allows to circulate inside the cave. Take pictures of the rind, but don't eat it unless you like a strong bitter flavor. The inside is quite grand, however, on a cracker or a crouton. A glass of Bourgogne Blanc makes a fine complement.

Sometimes Laini makes a third cut-off pyramid called Peppermid that is coated on the outside with black pepper. Again, the flavor is predictably much like the Valençay or Les Pyramides, but not surprisingly more peppery. When she's in the right mood, she makes both a Petite and a Gran Tomme, both very soft and smooth when young but maturing rapidly with age into a distinctive, not goaty flavor. Petite Tomme is a little larger than Capriola, a pleasantly fla-vored light brown round.

All of these cheeses are fully organic and are available on the Lazy Lady Farm outside Irasburg in the Northeast Kingdom. You will find these elegant cheeses on in several Vermont food coops as well as on cheese boards in several gourmet restaurants both in Vermont and in Boston. Except for the Capridos, all of her cheeses are small in size and quite expensive. The Lazy Lady has carved a unique and valuable niche for her products. There is nothing quite like them anywhere.

Goat Brie
KC's Kritters

This small, soft, approximately 8-ounce, 3½-inch disk, about ⅓ inch thick, is unique. Nowhere in the world, to my knowledge, will you find such a product. Nowhere will you experience such a deep, penetrating, even haunting flavor in a goat cheese, a flavor that only declares its identity long after the fact with just a faint ghost of goatiness at the back of the mouth. Smooth and creamy and perfectly white inside its edible cocoon of soft furry rind, its flavor far exceeds a mere physical sensation. If this sounds as if I am implying a spiritual dimension, I am.

It doesn't really matter what quality of white wine you serve with it because, like Vermont Shepherd, it will make almost any vintage taste elegant. If you're searching for the best, however, this is one of the few cheeses that will enhance a fine French champagne. Unfortunately it's not always available. But when it is, you'll find it at the

Brattleboro Food Coop in winter, and the Brattleboro Farmer's Market in summer.

FETA

The classic aged goat cheese is, of course, Feta. Most people think that it is made only from goat's milk, but the truth is that originally all Feta was made from sheep's milk. Now you will find Feta from all sorts of milk: goat's, sheep's, cow's, and for all I know yak's milk.

In Vermont you will find farmstead goat Feta from Does' Leap Farm in Bakersfield, KC's Kritters in Guilford, and Bonnie View Farm in Craftsbury. Does' Leap Feta is really best used in cooking because its Slavic style of preparation results in a much sharper and saltier product. In a quiche or on a pizza those strong qualities heighten the flavor without taking over the recipe. In a salad, however, its impact is best softened with a flavorful vinegar and a good virgin olive oil.

KC's Kritters' Feta is much less salty than any of the others. Kevin Kingsley cuts it into small cubes and packs it without brine into 8-ounce containers. It is therefore much drier than any of the other Fetas, but equally tasty.

And at Bonnie View Farms, Cheesemaker Victoria Von Hessert has finally come up with a fine sheep feta.

Flavored Goat Cheeses

There are several Vermont farmstead goat cheeses that mix garlic and herbs, even a light horseradish, in with the cheese. This practice originated in France with such soft, spreadable cheeses as Boursin, Valfrais, and Montrachet. The underlying edge that is natural to any fresh goat cheese blends strong flavors such as garlic, thyme, rosemary, basil, and cilantro into an attractive and harmonious spread.

KC's Kritters offers Swirls, two lightly aged soft goat cheeses. One has sun-dried tomatoes and basil rolled up in a thin layer of cheese, and the other features herbes de Provence spiraling attractively through the roll. In both cases the lemony flavor is distinctive, and the cheese is appealing sliced thin on crisp crackers or on a baguette. Both Swirls are attractively presented, although the color of the tomato-basil becomes blurred and smudgy looking as the cheese ages. Oddly, the flavor of the cheese improves as the appearance deteriorates.

Does' Leap has a Crottin (see Glossary) available that is basically the same combination of lightly aged goat cheese and herbs. Their organic milk definitely improves the flavor. Both the Swirl and the Crottin complement a cheese board with their appearance and their unusual flavor.

While we're thinking cheese board, Does' Leap makes two other uniquely attractive cheeses. Their Early Tomme is an Italian cheese with a pleasant but nondistinctive taste similar to the Gran Tomme of the Lazy Lady. They have also added a cheese they call Caprella that is simply exquisite. I don't think there is a goat cheese in the country that can touch this unique, silky satin, hauntingly flavored, white-rinded cheese. If you happen to have a bottle of 100-year-old Napoleon brandy in your cellar, it might enhance the quality of this cheese. Otherwise, don't clutter up the purity of its impact. You'll find it in the Onion River Coop in Burlington and the Burlington Farmer's Market. Does' Leap also makes a torta that will dress up any cheese board. This luxurious cheese is composed of alternate layers of basil and chèvre. It looks almost too good to eat, as the saying goes.

You can, of course, cook with all of the above cheeses if you wish, but it strikes me as a waste of superior cheese. Their principal appeal is cosmetic: they are a delight to the eye. If it's flavor you're after in some hot dish, you're better off with one of the many herb-flavored chèvres; if you need something stronger, use the plain Impastata from Vermont Butter and Cheese Company (see chapter 10) and add your own garlic and herbs.

Cheese molds lined up at Grafton Village Cheese Company

Nonfarmstead Cheeses

Some of Vermont's oldest and best-known cheeses are not made on farms. They come from various-sized cheese factories that have been manufacturing cheese for many years.

Vermont Butter and Cheese Company

The youngest of these is the Vermont Butter and Cheese Company just outside Barre, a stone's throw from the famous Vermont granite quarries. This company, which concentrates mainly on goat cheeses, produces nine high-quality products. Until the spring of 2001 it was eleven, but they were forced to drop two of their main claims to fame, a smoked salmon and

Mascarpone torta, and a basil and pine nut torta. Both were extravagantly decadent but proved to be so labor-intensive that the rest of their cheeses were suffering. The only way they could continue making them would be to lower their quality—and the company refused to do that.

Vermont Butter and Cheese makes a lot of special items such as fromage blanc, a creamy fresh cheese made from skim cow's milk that somehow contains no fat; crème fraîche, another French-style cultured cream that contains a lot of fat; Mascarpone, a super-rich pure white Italian cheese, a principal ingredient of *tiramisu* but also used in sauces, pastries, and fruit toppings; three goat chèvres, a plain, an herb, and one with pepper; and a lightly aged, soft ripened goat Chevrier. Their Goat Feta took a third-place ribbon in the 2001 American Cheese Society contest.

In addition to these, the company makes the following excellent gourmet cheeses:

GOAT FONTINA
Vermont Butter and Cheese Company

I doubt that there is another such cheese in the world. Vermont Butter and Cheese Company's Goat Fontina continues to be the star of their eclectic and prestigious lineup. This is an aged hard cheese with a strong distinctive signature. There is no hint of goat about its flavor, and it melts easily. Though it is quite low in moisture content, it doesn't feel dry when you taste it. In fact, it melts in your mouth. You will not soon forget this exceptional cheese, which comes in an 8- or 9-pound wheel that is about 2½ inches thick and a little more than a foot in diameter.

It was runner-up for Best of Show and first place in its own category at the U.S. Championship Cheese Contest in April 2001. This is a double compliment awarded by some of the discriminating judges in Wisconsin. Goat Fontina is also versatile. It is fine, for example, in cooked sauces—even better in fact than its famous Italian counterpart, which is normally considered the classic cooking cheese. Paired with a full-bodied Italian red wine or even one of California's fine Chardonnays, it is a meaningful experience.

The Fontina, along with many of Vermont Butter and Cheese's other products, can be found in several of the state's food coops as well as in such specialty food shops as the Cheese Trader in Burlington. You will often see it on the cheese boards of some of New York City's finest restaurants as well as many of the restaurants and inns of the New England Culinary Institute in Montpelier.

BONNE-BOUCHE
Vermont Butter and Cheese Company

A fairly recent addition, this won first place in the Aged Goat's Milk category of the American Cheese Society's competition in August 2001. Only slightly aged, Bonne-Bouche, which translates from the French as "good mouthful," is extraordinarily soft. There is the usual pure white of goat cheese shining through its attractive ash coating. The immediate impact of the first taste is a subtle but unmistakable hit of goat, which dissipates and disappears almost immediately, to be replaced by a mild, chèvrelike sweetness—almost as if you were tasting a Petite Suisse made from the milk of a goat instead of the usual cow.

These small, round, flat patties are naturals for a cheese board, either after or before dinner. Their almost liquid richness reminds me of a perfectly ripe Tumas d'la Paja from Italy or a last-stage Chaource from France. I don't think it's quite up to that rarefied level, but with a good Riesling or a white Zinfandel, it is an interesting cheese with an outstanding presentation. Look for it in gourmet restaurants both here in Vermont and in Boston or New York.

IMPASTATA
Vermont Butter and Cheese Company

Finally there are the three Impastatas. A little firmer than sour cream, lighter than Quark and cream cheese, the Plain Impastata has a nongoaty tanginess that is almost citruslike. Spread on a crisp cracker garnished with fresh chives or your favorite herbs, you will have the perfect summer accompaniment for your cucumber soup. There is also an Impastata made with ripe olives and another with roasted red peppers. Both are lovely to look at and pleasant to taste.

Grafton Village Cheese Company

The Grafton Village Cheese Company in Grafton, Vermont is a small factory that makes only Cheddar of various ages and flavors. Grafton uses only a raw Jersey milk that is guaranteed to be rBGH-free (see Glossary). In addition, all Grafton Cheddar is made by hand in the  same plant and by most of the same people who have been doing it for more than 40 years.

The company makes and markets a regular Red Label Cheddar, a Classic Black Label Cheddar, a three-year-old Gold Label Cheddar, and a four-year-old Four-Star Silver Label Cheddar. They also make a garlic and a sage variation, as well as a Maple Smoked Cheddar.

All of these Grafton Cheddars use a nonanimal microbial rennet (see The Rennet Quandary in the appendixes) for coagulating the raw milk, and all of them are available in food coops as well as major food stores and gourmet wine and cheese shops throughout New England. I have recently found some of them in the few mom-and-pop general stores still in existence. They are also available in color-coded waxed blocks, bricks, and wheels from 4 ounces up to 3 pounds. The regular is waxed in bright red, the Classic, Gold, and Four-Star in black wax, the smoked in brown, the sage in green, and the garlic in mahogany.

GRAFTON CLASSIC CHEDDAR
Grafton Cheese Company

This cheese has won so many prizes over the years that every knowledgeable tur-ophile in the nation knows about it. A soft, creamy interior, a mellow tartness, and an indelible individuality place it firmly at the top level of American Cheddars. The best ones are generally thought to come from England, where the name Cheddar originated, but this is not always true. English Cheddar is markedly different from American. It tends to be considerably harder, drier, and more pungent. *Lip-smacking* is the vernacular for their taste. American Cheddars, the best of which originate in Vermont, are softer, moister, and mellower. The only exception to this is Shelburne Farms cloth-wrapped Cheddar, which rivals the best of the English. Of course, it is arbitrary and completely personal to say that Keen's or Mont-gomery's Cheddar from England is "better" than Grafton's Classic—any more than you could boast that apples are better than oranges. They are so different from each other than any comparison is specious. Grafton's Classic can, however, be meaningfully compared with its recently introduced companion, Grafton Gold.

GRAFTON GOLD LABEL CHEDDAR
Grafton Cheese Company

This hauntingly sharp three-year-old Cheddar is remarkable. It deservedly won first place as the best Cheddar in the country at the American Cheese Society's competition in the summer of 2001. Its immediate impact, its soft mellowness, and its stunning flavor penetration are utterly amazing. This is unquestionably the finest Cheddar available in this country and should wear this crown proudly for several years to come. It is perhaps ironic that a glass of English port makes the perfect companion—though there may be a purist who will insist on sherry. In either case, the cheese is king.

Four-Star
Grafton Cheese Company

Grafton also offers a four-year-old Cheddar that bears the name Four-Star. It offers a slightly sharper edge than the Gold. There comes a point in many aged cheeses where their sharpness can easily slide into an overdose of saltiness or, perhaps even worse, into a vinegarlike sourness. The Four-Star flirts with that dangerous equilibrium, while the Gold is always steadily on the mark.

Smoked Cheddar
Grafton Cheese Company

In 1996 this cheese won first place in the Smoked Cheese Section of the American Cheese Society's annual competition. It was at best a pyrrhic victory, because no one with any knowledge of American cheese would argue that Grafton's Smoked Cheddar had ever been less than the best in the nation. It was only a matter of time before that was acknowledged and suitably trumpeted.

First of all, there is the strength and richness of a young classic Cheddar—which is then held from four to six hours over a so-called cool smoke from smoldering maple. "Cool" means that the smoldering damp wood and wood chips are in a separate room from the cheese; the smoke is piped in from a distance. By the time it gets there, it is cool. For those who delight in smoked cheese, the result is consistent and rich. For some reason when anyone says "smoked Cheddar" I start looking around for a dark ale or even a bottle of Porter.

CABOT CREAMERY

Asked to name Cheddar from Vermont, 9 out of 10 Americans will automatically answer "Cabot." Distributed all over the country and now beginning to show up in Europe, the many millions of pounds of various kinds of

Cheddar manufactured by the Cabot Creamery of Cabot, Vermont, cannot be ignored or passed over with a casual sneer as simply "supermarket cheese." It is true that all supermarkets carry Cabot Cheddar, but so also do many gourmet food shops.

There are a few excellent Cabot cheeses, which I will describe below.

Cabot is now making three organic Cheddars from organic milk furnished by Horizon, a nationally known collection of certified organic farms. Although there are Horizon organic dairy farms in Vermont, the Cabot cheeses do not claim to be made from their milk. They are making a mild, sharp, and extra-sharp Cheddar comparable in flavor to their nonorganic cheeses of the same name that are guaranteed rBGH-free.

Cabot, a dairy farmer cooperative, is wholly owned by Agri-Mark, a much larger Massachusetts-based farmer's coop, which also picks up and delivers its milk all over New England. Because there are so many dairy farms involved, it is impossible for Cabot to guarantee that there is no rBGH in their cheeses.

The good news is that all Cabot cheeses use vegetable enzymes as a coagulant. They do not use animal rennet. All but the extra-sharp are vacuum packed, and most are available in wax. All are made from pasteurized milk.

CABOT PRIVATE STOCK
Cabot Creamery

This is quintessential American Cheddar: soft, moist, and mellow. It is also quite sharp. If you like cheese on your popcorn, this is the one to use. Over the years it has alternated with Grafton and Shelburne Farms to win best Cheddar in the annual competitions. A smooth California red Zinfandel nicely complements its piquant flavor—and it melts well. Though it is not an elegant cheese, in a quiche or shirred eggs and omelets, even on a cheeseburger, it performs smoothly and positively.

Cabot Vintage
Cabot Creamery

Cabot Vintage is only available in wax and hardly differs from Private Stock. A sensitive and discerning palate may find it to be slightly mellower, a very little drier, and its flavor to last 27 seconds longer in the mouth. With its purple wrapping, it makes a nice gift for someone who is just beginning to appreciate cheese.

Cabot Extra Sharp
Cabot Creamery

This cheese is only extra sharp in the mind of the Cabot Division of Quality Control. There are two distinct kinds of Cheddar that carry the same label. One is made in 42-pound blocks and aged in a vacuum pack. The other is a 38-pound wheel, which is called a "flat," wrapped in cheesecloth and dipped in yellow wax and put in an attractive wooden box rather like an enlarged hat box and cured for up to three years. The former tastes much like Cabot Sharp, and the latter has a real bite to it. There is a degree of rawness about it, a little like the earlier versions of Cabot's Hunter Cheese. Cabot makes it specifically for small general stores whose trademark is a large wheel of Cabot cheese sitting on the counter under a bell jar to be custom cut as the customer wishes. It is not as sharp as Grafton Gold but it is headed that way. A pleasant table cheese with a noticeable kick to it.

Cabot Light Cheddar
Cabot Creamery

This cheese took first place in the Low Fat Category of the 2001 American Cheese Society's competition in Kentucky. I mention this cheese only because it is Cabot's gift to those lovers of cheese who are on stringent low-fat diets. This is one of the very few low-fat cheeses that has an acceptable flavor. While not sharp, it has a pleasant mild Cheddar taste and contains less than one-third of the fat content of normal cheeses.

Franklin County Cheese Company
Hahn's Cream Cheese

Hahn's is made from the rBGH-free milk of the St. Alban's Dairy Cooperative at the tidy, state-of-the-art Franklin County Cheese Company in northwestern Vermont. This old New York State recipe has been around for a long time and has proven itself reliable spread on a bagel, stirred into a dip, or baked into a cheesecake.

Plymouth Cheese Company

Plymouth Cheese doesn't really exist at the moment (see chapter 4). When it does reappear, as it most certainly will, it will be what it always was: simple, semisoft, pleasant, nondistinctive, and meltable. This Colby-type cheese is similar in texture to Crowley, in flavor to Orb Weaver. It will be made from pasteurized local cow's milk and sold principally at the Plymouth Cheese Company store in the tiny village of Plymouth in central Vermont.

CROWLEY CHEESE

Crowley Cheese has been around for longer than any other commercial cheese in the United States. Mr. Crowley made and sold his first wheel of cheese 123 years ago in the same building in Healdville, Vermont, where it is still made today.

Though there are no Crowleys associated with the company now, the cheese is the same and made in much the same way. At Crowley, the people will tell you that they don't make Cheddar and they don't make Colby: They make Crowley. Given the nature of this fine table cheese, this is an accurate description. Like the Extra Sharp Cheddar flat from Cabot, they wrap their 23-pound daisy wheel in cheesecloth and wax it with yellow wax. Their mild cheese ages for three months, their medium for six months, and their sharp at least a year. The latter is not subtle or pretentious. It states its case clearly and unequivocally, saying: "Try me. I am an old-fashioned table cheese that you can eat every day without getting bored. You can melt me, add me to your scrambled eggs, or wash me down with a cold beer on a hot summer day. I've been here a long time, and I'll always treat you right."

Crowley is made with animal rennet from raw milk guaranteed to be rBGH-free. It is available in 2½-pound wheels and bricks and a 23-pound daisy wheel in the Crowley Cheese Store on Route 103 in central Vermont, as well as in a number of food coops and local markets.

Italian Maremma sheepdogs patrol the flock at Mary Ella Farm

CHAPTER 11

The Future of Vermont Cheese

ERMONT IS ONE OF THE FEW PLACES IN THE COUN-
try where the old ways of doing things persist. There
are still one-cow farms. Workhorses, even oxen, still
work some of the fields. Not that they are any better. They are
simply more satisfying and more appropriate to Vermont's small,
rocky farms. Of course, new ways of accomplishing old things
come into being all the time.

What does this have to do with the state's young and vigor-
ous farmstead cheese industry? Where is it headed?

One harbinger of the future is the variety of different kinds
of cheese being produced in this state. In addition to all forms of
Cheddar, there is blue, Feta, Gorgonzola, Gruyère, Parmesan,
Fontina, Gouda, Swiss, Raclette, English-style, Brie, Camembert,

Mozzarella (both aged and fresh), Provolone, Caerphilly, Wensleydale, several sheep cheeses, more than a dozen goat cheeses and cream cheeses, and several more in development. When faced with the decision of what kind of cheese to make, new cheesemakers have to decide if it is to be unique to them or one that has proven market value. These are probably rhetorical questions because markets can be created, and it is already difficult to find a cheese that nobody else is making.

The large-scale cheesemakers are dependent on the supply of milk, which seems to have leveled off after years of shrinkage. Smaller dairy farms are looking for more profitable ways of using their milk, and cheese has become an increasingly common way to add value. Will this eventually bring to pass the vision of a cheesemaker in every town? Or a network of central aging and marketing facilities such as that now at Vermont Shepherd? Or a random increase of small, one-farm cheesemakers, each with its own facility and its own small collection of animals?

The answer is probably all of the above. Where proximity makes a pooling of resources cost- and energy-effective, centralized aging and marketing will appear, often with trained specialists to operate them. We will then see the appearance in Vermont of the *affineur,* one who knows how to cure cheese. Many cheesemakers are curing their own cheeses, but there are no trained, committed, full-time, professional *affineurs* here, as there are in England and France.

Independent loners will pop up in all corners of the state as various distributors enlarge their areas of pickup and delivery and as retailers seeking native and/or organic products either add new departments, enlarge old ones, or split off from the mainstream to create their own niches.

The steadily increasing number of food coops with an emphasis on healthy foods and local products are natural targets for farmstead cheese. Farmer's markets have become larger and more important in recent years, allowing cheesemakers to establish local reputations in line with the size of their outputs. For those who have enough production, there are the masters of fancy packaging: the catalogs, places such as Vermont Country Store or Williams-Sonoma. Finally there is the lure of the Internet as the next great commercial outlet.

There are many markets in many directions, and none of them is shrinking. For those interested in making a modest subsistence living, managing a limited farm operation that requires a relatively low financial investment, farmstead cheesemaking is an attractive opportunity. There are many challenges and there are many rewards.

And there are many problems still to be overcome, not the least of which is the problem of finding small-scale equipment that will pass the state regulations. And the problem of real estate: Many of the old stony farms have been bought up as summer homes for wealthy out-of-state families, and too often a beginning cheesemaker will be hard-pressed to find an appropriate, affordable farm. The germ of a solution to this and other problems is already planted in organizations such as the Vermont Cheese Council and the American Cheese Society.

Despite the recent closing of three of Vermont's small cheese factories, no matter how you throw the dice, the answer comes up the same: What is going on here in Vermont right now is the right people at the right time in the right place doing what they want to do and doing it well. Seldom does this happen, but with a little luck when it does, miracles are daily occurrences.

APPENDIXES

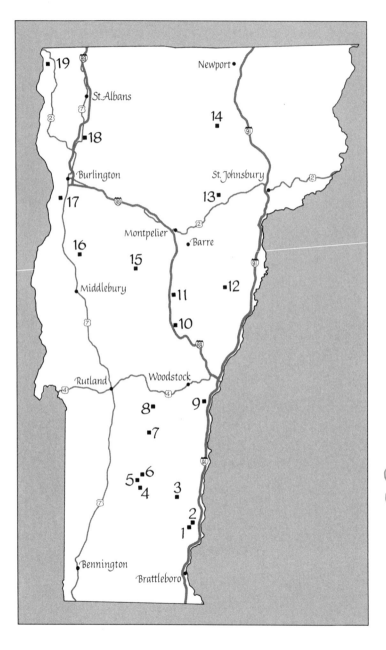

1. Westminster Dairy

2. Vermont Shepherd

3. Grafton Village Cheese Company

4. Pomeroy Farm

5. Taylor Farm

6. Woodcock Farm

7. Crowley Cheese Company

8. Plymouth Cheese Company

9. Cobb Hill Cheese Company

10. Karen Bixler

11. Neighborly Farms

12. Mary Ella Farm

13. Cabot Creamery

14. Bonnie View Farm

15. Three Shepherds of the Mad River Valley

16. Orb Weaver Farm

17. Shelburne Farms

18. Willow Hill Farm

19. Lakes End Cheese

Where to Find Vermont Farmstead Cheese

Farmstead Cheesemakers that Welcome Visitors
Addresses and Driving Directions

The following directions will take you right to the front door of all the cheese-makers in Vermont who welcome visitors. They ask only that you call first to be sure they will be available. All directions assume that you will be traveling north on I-91.

1. **Westminster Dairy**
   Peter Dixon
   Livewater Farm
   Westminster Road
   P.O. Box 0344
   Westminster, VT 05158
   802-387-5110

Take I-91 to exit 4 (Putney). Turn left at the end of the off ramp and continue into the village of Putney, then left onto Westminster Road at the General Store. Four or 5 miles past the junior high school is Livewater Farm on your left. If you reach Patch Road, you have passed it. Turn around, and it is the first farm on your right as you head back toward Putney. The cheese facility is right next to the barn behind the house.

2. **Vermont Shepherd**
   David and Cindy Major
   875 Patch Road
   Putney, VT 05346
   802-387-4473
   www.vermontshepherd.com

Vermont Shepherd is open to visitors four times a year. They have special cheese-tasting days for that specific purpose. Call to find out when they are, or consult the Vermont Shepherd web site (above). When you go there, take I-91 to exit 4 at Putney. Turn left off the off ramp and continue into the center of Putney, where you will find the General Store. Turn left there onto Westminster West Road. Follow this for at least 5 miles to Patch Road, which turns to the right under a large and beautiful willow tree. If you reach Westminster West, you have gone too far. On Patch Road, go past Patch Farm on your right. The next farm on the same side of the road at the top of a hill is the Vermont Shepherd. A small sign will inform you of that fact.

3. **Grafton Village Cheese Company**
   P.O. Box 87

Townshend Road
Grafton, VT 05146
1-800-472-3866
www.graftonvillagecheese.com
cheese@sover.net

Take I-91 north to exit 5 (Bellows Falls) and turn left at the bottom of the off ramp onto Route 121 west. Stay on 121 through Saxton's River into Grafton. Turn left at the Grafton Inn (which will be on your left) onto Townshend Road. Grafton Village Cheese Company is on your left less than .25 mile down this road. Their store is open 9–4 Monday through Friday. No need to call.

4. Pomeroy Farm
Jesse Pomeroy
R.R. 1, Box 12
Londonderry, VT 05148
802-824-3944

Take I-90 north to Brattleboro exit 2. Turn left from the off ramp onto Route 9. Stay on this into town. At the Main Street traffic light, follow signs to Route 30. Stay on Route 30 for a long time through Townshend. Pick up Route 100 in East Jamaica. Stay on Route 100 when it leaves Route 30 in Rawsonville. When you reach South Londonderry, let Route 100 continue on to your left while you stay on Middletown Road, over the bridge and up a steep hill perhaps 1.5 miles to a farm on your left. A sign proclaims it to be Middletown Farm. You have arrived.

5. **Taylor Farm**
   Katie and John Wright
   R.R. 1, Box 129
   Londonderry, VT 05148
   802-824-5690

Take I-91 north to Brattleboro exit 2. Turn left onto Route 9 east. Join Route 30 in the center of town at Main Street. Stay on Route 30 back out of town along the West River. Stay on Route 30 through Townshend and Jamaica. Turn right onto Route 100 north. Go through South Londonderry into Londonderry. Turn left onto Route 11 west. There is a shopping plaza at that junction. On the right 1 mile from that turn you will see a red barn and a gray house; a sign reads: TAYLOR FARM.

6. **Woodcock Farm**
   Gari and Mark Fischer
   10 Turner Road
   Weston, VT 05161
   802-824-6135

Take I-91 north to exit 6 (Rockingham). Turn left at the bottom of the off ramp onto Route 103 north. Stay on this until Chester, where you will meet Route 11.

Turn left onto Route 11 west to Londonderry, where you will meet Route 100. Do not go into town. Turn right onto Route 100 north as soon as you see it. After about 2 miles, you will pass the Frog's Leap Inn on your left. Turn right on the second driveway after the inn. If you go around a steep right-hand curve on Route 100, you have missed the drive. If you reach the town of Weston like I did, you have *really* missed the drive. Turn around and try again. Don't be discouraged because the drive looks like an abandoned gravel pit. That's what it is. Just past it you will drive right up to the cheese room and the Quonset barn attached to it.

7. **Crowley Cheese Company**
   Cindy Dawley (manager)
   Healdville Road
   Healdville, VT 05758
   802-259-2350

Take I-91 north to exit 6 (Rockingham). At the bottom of the off-ramp turn left onto Route 103, heading west toward Chester and Ludlow. After you pass through Ludlow, stay on Route 103, being careful that you don't get pulled off onto Route 100 north. About 6 miles past Ludlow, you will see the Crowley Cheese Store on your left. Almost immediately after that, a small sign on your left points to Healdville. Turn left over the railroad tracks and keep winding around, generally uphill, until you eventually reach the town. It's not far but the going is slow. The Crowley Cheese Factory is on your left at the top of the hill.

It is a very old-looking unpainted three-story building. There is a sign and a parking lot in front.

8. **Plymouth Cheese Company**
   P.O. Box 1
   Route 100A
   Plymouth, VT 05056
   802-672-3650

Take I-91 north to exit 6 (Rockingham). Turn left at the bottom of the off ramp onto Route 103 north. Stay on this through the town of Ludlow. Shortly after you leave Ludlow, Route 100 north comes in on your right. Take that and follow it for 8 or 9 miles into the town of Plymouth. Take Route 100A for 1 mile up the hill to Plymouth Notch. The cheese facility is on your left up the hill past the post office. As this book went to press in early 2002 the facility was not yet back in operation. Call for information on when it will reopen.

9. **Cobb Hill Cheese Company**
   Cedar Mountain Farm
   P.O. Box 134
   Mace Hill Road
   Hartland Four Corners, VT 05049
   802-436-1448

Take I-91 north to exit 9 (Hartland). Turn left at the bottom of the off ramp onto Route 5. Cross under the freeway into Hartland after only a few miles. Turn left onto Route 12 out of Hartland for a few miles into Hartland Four Corners. At the four corners, turn right onto Mace Hill Road and continue only .25 mile to the first farm on your left.

10. **Karen Bixler**
    R.R. 1, Box 408B
    Bethel, VT 05032
    802-234-6659

Take I-91 to I-89 north. Take exit 3 to Bethel. At the bottom of the exit ramp, turn right for .25 mile to a stop sign at a T. Turn left onto Route 14 for 2 miles. Route 14 curves to the right and a dirt road goes straight. This is Morse Road. Take it for 2 miles through a hard-to-see four corners (one road looks like a driveway). The second junction after that is a Y. Take the left branch; the first driveway on the right is Karen's farm, an old white farmhouse and new barn.

11. **Neighborly Farms of Vermont**
    Robert and Linda Dimmick
    1362 Curtis Road
    Randolph Center, VT 05061
    802-728-4700
    1-888-212-6898

www.neighborlyfarms.com
neighborlyfarms@quest-net.com

Turn off I-91 onto I-89 north and get off at exit 4 (Randolph). Turn right at the bottom of the exit ramp and drive about .5 mile to a T. You will see Vermont Technical College, a large white wooden building, across the road to your right. Turn left onto Route 66. When 66 makes a sharp right turn, continue straight ahead on Ridge Road. Proceed a little over a mile to North Randolph Road. Follow this well-maintained dirt road until you reach a four-corner intersection. You have arrived. The barn and cheese facility are on your left.

12. **Mary Ella Farm**
   Mary Ella and Harvey Carter
   4758 Chelsea Road
   Corinth Corners, VT 05039
   802-685-2058

Take I-91 north to exit 13, Thetford. At the bottom of the off-ramp, turn left onto Route 113 heading west. Follow 113 for about 15 miles until you reach Ward's Garage on the left. Turn right onto Goose Green Road. Stay on the asphalt, and in 2.5–3 miles you will pass Bob Osgood's Excavating on the left. The next farm on the left is Mary Ella Farm. Look for the sign.

13. Cabot Creamery
   Main Street
   Cabot, VT 05647
   800-837-4261
   www.cabotcheese.com
   info@cabotcheese.com

Take I-91 north to I-89 at White River Junction. Take I-89 north to Montpelier. Get off at exit 7 onto Route 62 and head past the hospital on your left, down the hill to Route 302, and finally to a traffic light at Route 2 at the bottom. Turn right onto Route 2 and stay on it through East Montpelier and Plainfield. When you come to Marshfield, opposite the General Store there is a road turning to your left called Marshfield Road or Route 215. Follow this road through Lower Cabot until you arrive in Cabot. The creamery is on your right—you can't miss it. The Cabot Visitors' Center is open seven days a week, 9–5, June through October. November through May the store is open 9–4 Monday through Saturday. The store is closed in January.

14. Bonnie View Farm
   Neil Urie
   2228 South Albany Road
   Craftsbury Common, VT 05827
   802-755-6878

Take I-91 past St. Johnsbury to exit 25 (Barton). Turn left under the freeway onto Route 16 west. After about 6 miles, you pass the second sawmill on your right, look for Mud Island Road, which is marked. Turn right and follow it until it dead-ends into a T composed of Massey Road on the left and Kinsey Road on the right. Turn right onto Kinsey Road (also called South Albany Road). The farm is about 2 miles down this road on your left. If you reach the village of South Albany, you have passed it.

15. **Three Shepherds of the Mad River Valley**
   Larry, Linda, Jackie, Heather, and Francis Faillace
   2193 Airport Road
   Warren, VT 05674
   802-496-3998

Take I-91 north to exit 6 (Rockingham). At the end of the off ramp, turn left under the freeway to Route 103 north to Ludlow. Shortly after passing through Ludlow, Route 100 north turns off to the right. Take it and follow it through the long valley, past the used cars and the cattle farm, and finally into Warren. Take the first right turn. Go through the small town and just before you leave it, Brook Road turns to your right. Take it and stay left on it until it reaches the top of the hill. There you will find the four corners of Roxbury Mountain. On your right when you stop at the intersection is a one-room schoolhouse. This is it. The cheese room is directly behind the school, which, of course, is now a store, not a school.

16. Orb Weaver Farm

Marjorie Susman and Marian Pollack
RD 1, Box 75
Lime Kiln Road
New Haven, VT 05742
802-877-3755
orbweaver@together.net

Take I-91 north to exit 2 in Brattleboro. Follow Route 9 west to Bennington. Pick up Route 7 north at Bennington. Stay on it through the town of Middlebury. About 7 or 8 miles north of Middlebury you will meet Route 17 at what is called New Haven Junction. Shortly afterward is Lime Kiln Road. Turn right and drive until you reach a stop sign at the junction of Lime Kiln Road and Plank Roads. Continue straight on Lime Kiln; the farm is the second on your right after the stop sign: a house, barn, and a greenhouse down from the road.

17. Shelburne Farms

1611 Harbor Road
Shelburne, VT 05482
802-985-8686
www.shelburnefarms.org

Go north on I-91 to White River Junction. Take I-89 north through Montpelier, continuing north until exit 13, just outside Burlington. The off ramp blends into a heavily traveled road and soon comes to a large intersection complete with traffic light. Try to get into the left lane before you reach the traffic light, because you should turn left at that light. This will put you on Route 7 south. Stay on that for 2.8 miles. At that point there should be a Volvo dealership on your left, and a narrow road called Bay Road turning off to your right. There is also a sign there announcing SHELBURNE FARMS. Turn right on that road and drive until you reach a gatehouse. They will direct you from there.

18. **Willow Hill Farm**
    Willow Smart
    313 Hardscrabble Road
    Milton, VT 05468
    802-893-2963
    www.sheepcheese.com

This is tricky, but you can do it. Take I-91 north to White River Junction, where you will get on I-89 north. Stay on I-89 through Montpelier and past Burlington, to exit 18. Take Route 7 south at the end of the off ramp. Stay on it past a long, lovely lake and over a bridge. After the bridge, take the first left onto Main Street, Milton, Vermont. There is a Mobil station there. A short distance later, you will cross some railroad tracks. Take the second right-hand turn after you cross the tracks. This will be East Road; there is a sign to tell you that. Less than .75 mile along East Road you should see a road going up a hill to your left; it does not have a sign. This is Hardscrabble Road. A sign reads

WILLOW HILL FARM. Take that road, and 1.4 miles later you will come to a large green barn set slightly down off the road on your right. There is a plastic-covered greenhouse next to it. This is Willow Hill Farm.

19. **Lake's End Cheese**
    Joanne James
    212 West Shore Road
    Alburg, VT 05440
    802-796-3730

Take I-91 to I-89 north at White River Junction. Take I-89 north through Burlington and get off on exit 17. Pick up Route 2 north and drive for 35 to 40 miles to Route 129 after you have crossed a long bridge. Follow Route 129 past the golf course. Then turn right at the Y and drive 2.5 miles to a sign on your right that reads SHORELINE CHOCOLATES. There may also be a sign by now that reads LAKE'S END CHEESE. The store is open 9–4 Monday through Saturday. No need to call.

Vermont Farmer's Markets and Food Coops (South to North)

Brattleboro Food Coop
2 Main Street/Brookside Plaza
Brattleboro, VT 05301
Phone: 802-257-0236
Fax: 802-254-5360
www.brattleborofoodcoop.com
bfc@sover.net
Open Monday through Saturday 8–9,
Sunday 9–9

Brattleboro Farmer's Market
Located on Route 9w, 1.5 miles from
Main Street (Route 5). Open Saturdays
10–2, May through October.

Londonderry Farmer's Market
At the junction of Routes 100 and 11 just
before you reach Londonderry. Open
Saturdays 9:30–2:30, May through
October

Putney Food Coop
P.O. Box 730
Main Street

Putney, VT 05346
Phone: 802-387-5866
Fax: 802-387-2350
Open Monday through Saturday 7:30–8,
Sunday 8–8

Upper Valley Food Coop
193 N. Main Street
White River Junction, VT 05001
802-295-5804
Open Monday through Saturday 9–8,
Sunday 11–7

Norwich Farmer's Market
Located on Route 5, 1 mile south of
Norwich. Open Saturdays 9–1, May
through October.

Hanover (N.H.) Food Coop
45 South Park Street
Hanover, NH 03755
603-643-2667
Open 8–8 seven days a week

Lebanon (N.H.) Food Coop

Centerra Marketplace
Route 120
Lebanon, NH 03766
603-643-4889
Open daily 7–9

Rutland Area Food Coop

77 Wales Street
Rutland, VT 05701
802-773-0737
rafe@juno.com
Open Monday through Saturday 9–7

Middlebury Natural Foods Coop

1 Washington Street
Middlebury, VT 05753
Phone: 802-388-7276
Fax: 802-388-4817
Open 8–7 seven days a week

Middlebury Farmer's Market

Located at the MarbleWorks, a small area
behind Main Street in downtown
Middlebury. Open Saturdays 9–12,
May through October.

Mad River Valley Farmer's Market

Waitsfield Center. Open Saturdays 10–2,
May through October

Hunger Mountain Food Coop

623 Stonecutters Way
Montpelier, VT 05602
802-223-6910
Open daily 8–8

Adamant Coop

Adamant Road
Adamant, VT 05640
802-223-5760
Open Monday through
Friday 9:30–6; Saturday 9:30–3;
Sunday 10–1

Onion River Coop

274 North Winooski Avenue
Burlington, VT 05401
802-863-3659
onionriv@aol.com
Open Monday through
Saturday 9:30–8,
Sunday noon–5

Cheese Traders

1186 Williston Road
South Burlington, VT 05403
802-863-0143
Open 10–7 Monday through
Saturday

Burlington Farmer's Market
Located in City Hall Park in downtown
Burlington. Open Saturdays 8:30–2:30,
May through October.

Buffalo Mountain Food Coop
Main Street
Hardwick, VT 05843
802-472-6020
Open Monday through Thursday 9–6;
Friday 9–7; Saturday 9–6; Sunday 10

National Sources of Vermont Farmstead Cheese

Vermont farmstead cheeses are available online from the Vermont Cheese Council at www. vtcheese.com, and in Bread & Circus and Whole Foods supermarkets nationwide. You'll also find Vermont farmstead cheeses at the following retail outlets:

Dean & Deluca, 560 Broadway, New York City

Fairway Market, 2127 Broadway at 74th Street, New York City

Murray's Cheese Shop, 257 Bleecker Street, New York City; murrayscheese@ msn.com

Zabar's, 2245 Broadway, New York City

Formaggio Kitchen, 244 Huron Avenue, Cambridge, Massachusetts

Zingerman's Deli, 422 Detroit Street, Ann Arbor, Michigan

Organizations

Vermont Cheese Council

Dawn Morin-Boucher, President
116 State Street, Drawer 20
Montpelier, VT 05620-2901
1-888-523-7484
www.vtcheese.com
info@vtcheese.com

American Cheese Society

P.O. Box 303
Delavan, WI 53114-0303
502-583-3783
www.cheesesociety.org

Vermont Department of Agriculture

Dairy Section
116 State Street
Montpelier, VT 05602-2901
1-800-295-9873

Publications

Code of Best Practices

This comprehensive guide for Vermont cheesemakers is published by the Vermont Department of Agriculture (see contact information above). Also available from the Vermont Cheese Council (see left).

Vermont Cheese Council Newsletter

The Vermont Cheese Council
116 State Street, Drawer 20
Montpelier, VT 05620-1901
1-888-523-7484
www.vtcheese.com

Farmstead Cheesemaking

(quarterly journal)
Peter Dixon
P.O. Box 993
Putney, VT 05346

Phone: 802-387-4803
Fax: 802-463-9440
Pdixon@together.net

INSTRUCTION AND SUPPLIES

Peter Dixon runs frequent workshops for aspiring cheesemakers. Call or write at the address above for a current schedule.

Paul Kinstedt offers 3-day courses in farmstead cheesemaking twice a year at the University of Vermont. They are typically sold out; contact the University of Vermont for information on upcoming classes.

New England Cheesemaking Supply Company
Rickie Carroll
Ashfield, MA 01330
413-628-3808
www.cheesemaking.com

The Rennet Quandary

The apocryphal tale that is usually told about the origin of cheese is that some post–Stone Age man who wanted to carry some milk on a trip put it in a calf stomach that he happened to have lying around. When he got to his destination, he discovered that he didn't have milk anymore . . . he had cheese in the stomach. Could be true. Rennet does indeed come from the lining of the fourth stomach of a calf.

A large hue and cry from the animal rights people has resulted in the invention of several other microbial coagulants that will solidify milk into curds for making cheese:

1. There is a fungal enzyme called chymosin taken from the mold in a fermentation vat. This is not genetically modified.

2. When you add a gene from a cow to the above mold, the DNA is identified as either Fermentation Derived Chymosin or Fermentation Produced Chymosin. This has been genetically modified.

The terms *vegetable coagulants, vegetable enzymes,* and *vegetable rennet* all refer to one of the above molds. All molds are considered vegetables.

In Spain and Portugal, there is rennet available from a thistle plant, but it is not available in this country.

There are major disagreements among cheesemakers about the importance of using animal rennet versus vegetable coagulant. What is certain, however, is that the animal rights activists, as well meaning as they are, have been fighting a battle that doesn't exist. No calf was ever butchered solely in order to get rennet. Rennet is a by-product of the veal industry.

How to Read Cheese Labels

Federal regulations require that cheesemakers list the nutrients in all their products, and many of the larger high-profile cheesemakers comply. It is not a regulation that is taken seriously, however, and is not very well enforced. Since most farmstead cheesemakers are working close to the break-even point, they seldom squander the time and money to do the research.

For all cheesemakers, however, the label is primarily a marketing device. They spend endless amounts of time and money to come up with a seductive name for each cheese and then to describe it as attractively as possible on the label. The result of all this sales creativity is that the labels are not completely accurate. They more often reflect wishful thinking than hard facts. For example, since it is a common belief among those who make Cheddar that most people are attracted to a "sharp" cheese, they will use the word loosely, marking in bold print the word *sharp* when in actuality it is more likely to be medium. Most Cheddars marked "extra sharp" are in fact only sharp at the most. The words *sharp, extra sharp, medium,* and *mild* are truly indicative only of the age of the cheese. They have nothing to do with content. A more appropriate statement will tell you, the buyer, how long a cheese has been aged; some cheesemakers actually will include that information on their labels.

Following are a couple of useful rules of thumb for the innocent buyer:

1. Whatever the label says about sharpness, mentally back it up one degree. In other words, if it says "sharp," change it in your mind to "medium." If it says "medium," change it to "mild."

2. Roughly speaking, it takes six months to a year of aging to make a cheese sharp, and two to three years to make it extra sharp. After that, you're in no-man's-land. It often happens that a cheese aged four or five years is actually not much sharper than the one aged two or three. And there are a few Cheddars that come out consistently and mouthwateringly sharp after only a year of aging. You just have to experiment until you find one that appeals to you.

There is one part of the label that is accurate by definition: the nutritional breakdown (if there is one). Nearly all breakdowns are predicated on a 1-ounce sample. If, for example, the label reads "12–14 grams saturated fat," it means there are 12 to 14 grams of saturated fat in a 1-ounce sample. That is about average for a whole-milk cheese. Low-fat cheese generally runs from 7 to 9 grams, with some as low as 2.5 grams. Salt content, which is expressed in milligrams, is recorded as sodium, with 200 to 225 milligrams being the average per ounce. There is at least one well-known cheese with only 50 milligrams of sodium, and it has an excellent flavor in spite of that.

Many other ingredients are also expressed in percentages for the further edification of the knowledgeable buyer. A "14 percent calories from fat" reading corresponds closely to 12 to 14 grams of saturated fat.

In addition to the colorful marketing label, which generally includes the above information as well as a note telling you whether the cheese is made with rennet or enzymes and whether or not the milk has been pasteurized, you will find a cost label that repeats the name of the cheese and includes the weight and total price of this particular piece and its price per pound, as well as the date on which it was packed. It pays to check cost labels because they often contain errors in price and weight that are usually human in origin—but may reflect computer glitches that can furnish wild inaccuracies to confuse the already somewhat mystified buyer.

Most prepacked cheeses, meaning those that are packaged by the manufacturer and not by the individual store, have somewhere on their labels a stamped date, called the sell-by date. These are characteristically hard to locate and often even more difficult to read. They are for the most part pretty conservative, and you can almost always count on a couple of weeks beyond the date if you don't open the package. Most reputable cheese departments will not put out any cheese past its sell-by date, but it pays to check it out since it's hard to keep track of all the dates in a display case.

Some Customer Rights and Wrongs

In all cheese departments that wrap and label a portion of their products in the store, you can ask for tastes of any cheeses that attract you. Most stores will be happy to comply, and in fact many will have various cheeses available for tasting. You should also feel free to ask any questions about the cheeses you see and those you are looking for but can't find. The main problem is finding someone to take care of you. Supermarket cheese departments are usually poorly staffed, and finding someone who is knowledgeable about their products can be frustrating.

You have the right to pick up any product in the display case and examine it closely without damaging it. You can smell it, too, although this is pretty much a futile exercise with today's tight plastic wrapping. But old customs die slowly, and you will still see people sniffing away at plastic-wrapped cheese and acting as if they actually smelled something.

acidity: Like soils, cheeses are affected by how acidic or alkaline they are. Lactic acid forms in cheese as the milk warms. The level of acidity is controlled by the addition of salt.

affineur, affineuse: One who dedicates his or her whole professional time to aging, curing, and taking care of cheese.

bulk tank: A large metal tank usually made of stainless steel where milk is stored until it is either picked up by a dairy or used for making cheese.

calving: The process of birthing a calf from a cow.

can cooler: An insulated container that is equipped with refrigeration. These are usually large enough to walk into, although they are often top-opening, waist-high.

cave: A room or a chamber dug out or constructed underground in which the temperature and humidity can be carefully controlled over a long period of time.

cheddaring: The process of cutting the curd into slabs after most of the whey has been drained off. The slabs are piled up and turned several times before they are milled.

cheese facility: Any collection of adjoining rooms equipped and dedicated to the manufacture of cheese. Generally includes at least a special room where the cheese is made, a refrigerated storage room, and a brining tank. Often in the case of goats and sheep, the facility will also include a milking parlor where the actual milking of the animals takes place.

cheese vat: A stainless-steel tank or vessel in which the milk is transformed into cheese. Most of them have jackets surrounding them in which steam or hot water can be circulated in order to raise the temperature of the milk to the desired level.

chèvre: Means "goat" in French. Hence, it is used in many forms to identify several soft fresh goat cheeses. Hard goat cheeses are often referred to as aged chèvres.

coagulant: A substance added to milk that separates the milk into solids and liquids, so-called curds and whey (see The Rennet Quandary).

crottin: A small, round, soft goat cheese; larger than a button, smaller than a tomme.

cultures: Any one of several mixes of live bacteria that affect the taste and texture of the cheese. Cultures can be made in your own kitchen, or purchased from a cheesemaker's supply company (see Resources and Information).

curd: A soft solid remaining after the liquid whey is poured off. Most of the milk protein is in the curd, which can be eaten and is indeed available commercially. In the 1920s a bowl of salted curd decorated most bars to accompany the beer.

de-horning: Cutting the horns off various dairy animals. It is a common belief among many dairy farmers that their animals, which spend a great deal of their lives in a barn, can injure themselves and those around them with their horns. Usually a job for a large-animal veterinarian.

distributor: A wholesale company that buys products from manufacturers and sells them to retail stores and other distributors. In the process, they distribute the products over whatever area they choose to serve. In the Vermont farmstead cheese business, they pick up products from the farm and sell them to retail cheese outlets.

DNA: That part of the genetic system of an animal that organizes and arranges the growth of cells programmed to accomplish their assigned tasks in the construction of the completed organism. The double helix discovered by Watson and Crick almost half a century ago became the basis for DNA research and today's research into human and animal genomes.

enzymes: Webster calls them "complex proteins produced by living cells that catalyze specific biochemical reactions at body temperature." In cheesemaking they are used instead of rennet to separate the curds from the whey (see The Rennet Quandary).

fermentation: The transformation of an organic compound by the addition of enzymes. Example: transformation of hard cider into vinegar. Cheese passes through a period of fermentation as it ages and becomes drier and harder.

free-stall: A barn without stanchions in which the animals are permitted to move about without restriction is called a free-stall barn.

freshen: When a female dairy animal has a calf, she lets down her milk so that her newborn can begin to nurse. This process is called freshening.

genetically modified: Sometimes referred to as genetically engineered. This is a natural product whose genes have been changed in some way that will benefit the grower or the manufacturer of the item. For example: Soybeans have been modified to resist certain invasions of unfriendly insects so that the growers do not need to use insecticides. Although there is no documented evidence of harmful side effects traceable to this process, this practice has so far been outlawed in Great Britain and the European Union.

kid: A young goat. They are generally called kids until they are old enough to breed.

lambing: The process of birthing lambs. Mostly, the sheep can handle this by themselves but sometimes they need assistance.

milking parlor: A room in the barn devoted specifically to the milking of whatever dairy animal is raised there.

milking stand: A small platform used mainly for goats. The doe jumps up on the platform, puts her head through a stanchion, and eats her grain while she is being milked.

name controlled: The governments of certain countries (such as France, England, and Denmark) protect the names of certain of their best-known national cheeses. These cheeses are forbidden by law to be made anywhere in the world except in a closely described area in the host country. The methods and materials of making the cheese must also pass stringent inspection and be maintained for the highest quality.

organic: It has taken the U.S. Department of Agriculture more than two years to come up with a satisfactory definition of this term. Simply, it means using only natural means of growing any animal, fish, or vegetable product. In practice, this means no chemical fertilizers in the fields and no manufactured additives to the feed. Also it means no pesticides, no herbicides, no fungicides, and no man-made pharmaceuticals used either in the fields or on the animals. If you want a boring way to spend an evening, go on the Internet to the USDA web site and punch in the word *organic.* You will be amazed if not instructed.

pasteurize: The process of heating milk to a temperature high enough to destroy objectionable bacteria without altering the other ingredients of milk too much. This is accomplished in a pasteurizer, which is essentially a kettle specially designed to heat the milk to an exact temperature and hold it at that temperature for a specified length of time. There is a major movement afoot in the USDA to require that all milk for public consumption, including that used to make cheese, be pasteurized. There is an equally major movement among farmers, cheesemakers, and consumers to defeat this idea. So-called raw milk is in high demand in certain areas, and raw milk cheeses are much sought after.

pavé: We all know what this word means in English, but in French, with an accent over the *e*, it refers to the shape of a piece of cheese. A *pavé* is shaped like a small square paving stone.

pecorino: This is the Italian word for "sheep" and is used mainly in connection with certain Italian cheeses made from sheep's milk, such as Pecorino Romano and Pecorino Ricotta.

pitching: Another term for "cheddaring."

raw milk: Milk that has not been pasteurized.

rBGH: Translated from chemical jargon into English, these letters stand for recombinant "bovine growth hormone." This is an artificial growth hormone developed and patented by the Monsanto Chemical Company. It comes in the form of a very expensive injection that is used to inoculate producing cows in order to significantly increase the amount of milk they give.

Monsanto claims that there are no harmful side effects, but anecdotal evidence of birth defects, infertility, and shortened life expectancy in the animals that have been treated has made many of Vermont's dairy farmers nervous about using it. The U.S. Department of Agriculture has signed off on rBGH as being harmless for human consumption, though there are many who think it has not been available for long enough to produce thorough and authentic results.

rennet: A substance found in the lining of the fourth stomach of a calf. It is used to separate the curds from the whey when making cheese (see The Rennet Quandary).

rind: The outer skin of a piece of cheese that has been exposed to the air during the process of aging. It is often darker and drier than the inside of the cheese and tends to be not so flavorful. There is nothing harmful about eating the rind. In soft cheeses such as Brie or Camembert, for example, it will actually improve the taste of the cheese.

rotation grazing: This is a method of pasture management in which the farmer moves her or his animals from one pasture to another on a regular schedule. Depending upon how often this is done—sometimes two or three times in one day—the pasture is kept from overgrazing.

scalding: The process of heating milk to a temperature just below the boiling point.

separator: A very expensive piece of machinery that automatically separates the cream from the milk. This is used in making butter and in all low-fat and part-skim operations.

stanchion: Originally made of wood but now entirely of metal, this ingenious device locks the milking animal's head loosely in place so that it can eat what is put in front of it while it is being milked. In many barns, the animals are kept in stanchions all the time so that they will not mess up the barn unduly.

steer: A a steer is a castrated bull.

tome, tomme, tuma: When used in connection with cheese, these words refer to its shape and size only. Usually, the word describes a fairly flat wheel no more than 8 inches in diameter, although there are flat square Italian cheeses called tumas.

torta: A soft, rich cheese made in layers. Usually made with Mascarpone alternating with gourmet items such as smoked salmon, leeks, basil, sun-dried tomatoes, and so on.

turophile: A lover of cheese.

washed-rind: These are usually farmstead wheels that have been carefully dipped or washed with everything from beer to wine or even honey during the process of aging. They are commonly thinner, flatter wheels than those that have been aged without washing. Some most interesting flavors are created in this manner.

whey: The liquid part of milk that has been separated from the curds. There is practically nothing in it except water although, with a lot of effort, there are some cheeses made from it. Most often it is fed to pigs or sprayed on the fields for fertilizer.